Letters to Josep

An Introduction to Judaism

Daniella Levy

Copyright © 2016 by Daniella Levy

All rights reserved. This book or any portion thereof may not be reproduced or used in any manner whatsoever without the express written permission of the publisher except for the use of brief quotations in a book review.

Design elements from the Vectorian FreeVector Pack (www.vectorian.net) were incorporated into this book. They are licensed under a CreativeCommons Attribution 3.0 Unported License.

First Printing, 2016

ISBN 978-965-92540-0-2

Guiding Light Press
P.O. Box #505
Tekoa, D.N. North Judea 90908
Israel

*I am honored to dedicate this book
in loving memory of two women
whose contributions to it were not direct,
but were nonetheless essential.*
My grandmother,
Seena Kronenberg Baker
1930—2015
and Josep's grandmother,
Maria Pilar Chisbert i Gimeno, a.k.a. Vicenteta
1925—2009

Table of Contents

Foreword..6
How It All Began..10

Observant Jewish Life..17

   The Basics..18
   An Introduction to the World's Biggest Book Club........20
   Shabbat: A Sacred Space in Time....................................26
   Jew Food, Part I: Vegetarians, Avert Your Eyes..............36
   Jew Food, Part II: The Vegetarian Section (Well, Sort Of)..44
   Jew Food, Part III: In Which Things Get Ridiculously Complicated..50
   Prayer, Part I: Why Pray?..56
   Prayer, Part II: A Peek into the Jewish Prayer Book......60
   Mikveh: A Spiritual Womb..68
   Circumcision. Wait! Don't Run Away Screaming!.........76
   On the Doorposts of Your Home: All About Mezuzot..82
   Blessings: Finding God in an Apple................................88
   Jewish Weddings..94
   Processing Grief: Jewish Mourning Customs................102
   Jewish by Choice: The Ins and Outs of Halakhic Conversion..110
   Women in Orthodox Judaism, or: Daniella Opens a Can..118

The Jewish Year..127

   The Jewish Year..128
   Your Personal Jewish Calendar......................................130
   Days of Awe..134
   In God's Presence: Succot & Shmini Atzeret................144
   Let There Be Light..150
   Purim: Divine Hide-and-Seek..154

Table of Contents

Passover, Part I: Freedom, Education, and National Obsessive-Compulsive Disorder 158
Passover, Part II: Seder Night 101 162
In the Empty Synagogues of Poland 170
Israeli Emotional Roller Coaster Week 174
Counting Up: The Omer and Lag B'Omer 180
Why Jerusalem Matters 186
Shavuot: On Covenants and Cheesecake 194
Starving for God: Jewish Fast Days 200
Between the Dire Straits 206

Jewish Concepts 213

Different Kinds of Jews, Part I: Jewish Cultural Identity and the Diversity Therein 214
Different Kinds of Jews, Part II: 2,000 Years of Arguing 222
Happily Ever After: The Jewish Messiah 232
A Nation of Pyromaniacs 236
Teshuva: As Long as the Candle Burns 242
Jewish Symbols 248
The Sabbath Keeps the Jews... Even When It Seems like It Doesn't 252
Links in the Chain: On Educating Children 256
The Vagueries of the Jewish Afterlife 260
The Battleground of Good and Evil 266
Crossing Boundaries 272
I Forgave God 276

Appendices 283

Acknowledgements 286
A Little Catalan Context 284
Glossary 286
About the Author 291

5

Foreword

WHEN I MET DANIELLA in October of 2006, I was in my last year of study at the Autonomous University of Barcelona, earning a Political Science degree with a specialization in International Relations and European Studies. I was working as an intern at the United Nations Association of Spain (ANUE in the Catalan acronym)—a highly coveted position that I was very lucky to get.

By that time, at age twenty-four, I was somewhat familiar with the tragedies of the Jews throughout the history of humankind. Like most young teenagers, we were taught contemporary history in high school, which included a very comprehensive review of the Second World War and some details about the Holocaust. Also, when I was twelve, Spielberg's *Schindler's List* was released in the cinemas of Barcelona, and my professors decided that the whole school should see it and made a day trip out of it. That story of the senseless bloodshed of a group of innocent human beings had stuck with me since then. And that, along with my passionately reading anything that bore the name of Sir Winston Churchill or concerned the Second World War, meant that I was very familiar with the Shoah, but I had yet to meet a real Jew. Daniella was the first.

Additionally, I was developing some curiosity about my Converso surnames. Of my eight grandparents, three-and-a-half of their surnames turned out to be of Converso origin, so I really wanted to learn more about Judaism. I had also started to work on a book about the Arab-Israeli conflict around that time. I wanted to explore the issue in depth, but never found a comprehensive book that described the whole picture. So I decided to write one myself. And how can you write about something that you do not know?

So when Daniella and I ended up together on the international press team for a conference organized by ANUE, I had a particular interest in getting to know her a little bit deeper than the rest of the team. I wanted to learn more about Judaism, but did not want to make a big deal out of her identity as a Jew. I did not want her to think that I was defining her as a person by it. As a liberal, religion has always been a private thing for me. Nonetheless, we started talking and getting to know each other, and as we did, I was astonished to learn that the United Nations Association was not considering Daniella's religious needs, such as gender-segregated sleeping arrangements and kosher food. I knew nothing about kosher food, but I tried everything I could to help her. The United Nations Association, by contrast, could not have cared less. I took personal offense at this. As a Catalan, it was important to me that every visitor to my country be treated properly, especially at a United Nations event! But Daniella was touched by my concern and noticed my genuine interest in Judaism, and thus, our friendship was born.

I really cannot recall how our correspondence began, but I distinctly remember Daniella trying to help me to get in touch with my Jewish roots once she was back home. One of the first things I can recall is her putting me in contact with a woman named Gloria—the researcher who founded the Casa Shalom Institute for Marrano-Anusim Studies. It was really sweet of her, and while it was helpful, I remember being really reluctant to try and get information about our Jewish roots from my grandmother, who was a devoted Catholic and had attended service almost daily since she was a child. How do you bring this up with your sweet grandma: "Hey, Iaia, why did you sing *Hava Nagila* when you played as a child and teach it to your daughters?" Not an easy task!

Daniella always has been and always will be a writer, and my interest in Judaism and Israel really brought that out in her. For some reason, she decided that it was part of her mission to help me understand Judaism better and what it means to be a Jew in the 21st century. We started exchanging regular emails in which she would explain to me about her daily life, relating to the Jewish festivals, holidays, or traditions. I would ask her about aspects of the faith that were totally unknown to me. We would frequently compare Judaism to Christianity to expose the differences between them, without prior prejudices in either of us.

But, obviously, she has always been the teacher and I have always been the student. She is far more knowledgeable about interfaith relations, and indeed about Catholicism, than I am. I have always faced my relationship with God from my own personal experience rather than relying on tradition or the Church hierarchy. Daniella has always been afraid of being too pushy or that I might get offended because of the inherent conflict between Judaism and Christianity, but I have never felt that way. Knowledge and criticism have never offended me. On the contrary!

But far from always focusing on religion, our correspondence would also concern events in both our countries and in the world in general. Antisemitism has always been a frequent topic of discussion, as Europe is culturally prone to antisemitism—not that anyone would admit that; and this is something I have been very adamant to fight. It makes my skin itch to still have to explain to perfectly functioning adults that antisemitism is racism, and that being against the existence of Israel is a modern form of antisemitism.

It has always been a challenge for me to keep up with Daniella's prolific e-mails. Judaism has so many traditions and celebrations—and so many different points of view and debates within those traditions. She would try to explain all of this to

Foreword

me. It would take me a month to get an answer to her... and then she would respond in twenty-four hours or less!

Despite this imbalance and the frequent ups and downs in the decade we have known each other, to her credit, Daniella has always been very persistent in maintaining our friendship. She was always very creative in trying to keep us close and in touch. We have had periods when our communication was non-existent and others when we would communicate on an almost daily basis. The blog *Letters to Josep* was one of her imaginative solutions. She created it in order to take the pressure of reading and responding off of me, so that I could enjoy those e-mails when I had the time, and she could go on writing them whenever she liked without worrying it would overwhelm me.

Daniella always treats everyone with love and respect, and she has been a very loyal friend to me. It is an honor and a blessing that someone like Daniella has chosen me to be her friend and the recipient of all of her wisdom.

Finally, I would like to tell you, dear reader, that you are about to embark on something more than a book. You are about to participate in a quest for friendship, understanding, and love, beyond languages, religion, and borders. I do hope that you will find yourself the recipient of the wisdom Daniella has tried to impart to me. But I really hope that, beyond wisdom, you'll also find part of the love I have received from Daniella.

"Josep"
Barcelona, September 2015

How It All Began

~~~~~~~~~⊙~~~~~~~~~

BARCELONA, CATALONIA, SPAIN. OCTOBER, 2006. I stepped out of the airport shuttle at Plaça de Catalunya and looked around to get my bearings, dragging a wheeled suitcase behind me. This was not my first trip to Europe, nor was it my first time traveling internationally without my parents; but this *was* my first time traveling to a foreign country completely on my own. I was nineteen years old, in my second year of national service.[1] A writer since I figured out how to hold a pen, I'd been part of an online community of teen writers for a while, and the friend who ran that community had invited me to join the press team she was heading for an international youth conference in Barcelona. I was delighted to accept.

Now, at this point, there are a few important things you should know about me. One: I am not the "reporter" type. Shy, introspective, and quiet, I am the last person you would expect to burst into a room full of people and start interviewing somebody. Two: I am an observant Jew. That means that I adhere

---

[1] National service, *sherut leumi*, is an alternative to compulsory military service, for people who can't or won't serve in the IDF for health-related, religious, or moral reasons. Many young women from my community prefer this alternative because it is a far more comfortable environment for religious women than the army. I have plenty of religious female friends who served in the IDF as well.

strictly to Jewish law in every aspect of life, from keeping kosher (the dietary laws) to abstaining from all work and "acts of creation" on the Sabbath. Before my trip, the editor-in-chief had assured me that my religious needs would be accommodated: that kosher food would be available; that our room at the youth hostel would be girls-only; and that no work would be required of me on Saturday. Still, I am not ashamed to admit that I grew up in a bubble—a warm, lovely, fulfilling bubble, but a bubble nonetheless.

In short, I was roughly 2,000 miles from my comfort zone.

One more important thing you need to know about me before we proceed is that ever since reading Naomi Ragen's *The Ghost of Hannah Mendes* as a young teen, I have had an inexplicable obsession with the Spanish Inquisition and the concept of crypto-Judaism. I had, in fact, made friends with someone in the US who believed that she was descended from crypto-Jews. I was very involved in her exploration of Judaism and her journey to pursue her Jewish heritage. This passion gave traveling to Barcelona another level of meaning for me.

That first day, I found my room at the hostel, and as soon as I'd settled in, I headed right back out to search for the old Jewish Quarter, the "Call." I found it and poked around the ancient synagogue, and then headed in the other direction to find the only kosher store in the city, hoping to find some options for food for the Sabbath. It was Wednesday, and I didn't know if I'd have access to a refrigerator. I was told that the following day there were challahs[2] and other Shabbat necessities sold, so I resolved to come back then. In the meantime, I bought a bottle of grape juice and headed back to the hostel.

The editor-in-chief and the graphic designer, both from America, were waiting there for me. Toward evening, we went down to the sidewalk in front of the hostel, where we were introduced to the rest of the press team. They were all locals, some of whom had been recruited at the last minute due to

---

[2] Challah—the special bread for the Sabbath. See *Shabbat: A Sacred Space in Time*.

budget cuts that had forced some of the other international members of the press team to cancel. When I was introduced to the group as "Daniella, from Israel," one of these last-minute local recruits looked at me with wide eyes.

"You're from Israel?" he asked.

I sized him up apprehensively. Europe, in general, is known for being hostile toward Israel, and Barcelona has, at times, been considered one of the most antisemitic cities in Europe. I had been warned not to wear anything outwardly Jewish and to keep my nationality discreet. Heart pounding a little, I answered that, yes, I was.

"I was supposed to be there this summer!" he exclaimed. "The trip was canceled at the last minute. I even had the tickets..."

Well, that didn't sound like the beginning of an anti-Israel tirade.

Relieved, I laughed and said, "Well, I can understand why you didn't end up coming..." The Second Lebanon War was in July of that year. You'd be surprised how many trips to Israel ended up under the category of "Canceled on Account of Rockets."

I squinted at him questioningly. "Why... what's your connection to Israel?" I ventured.

He answered that he was Roman Catholic, but had always been fascinated with Israel and Judaism, and as the group began moving down the sidewalk, we found ourselves deep in conversation. As it turned out, he was a die-hard fan of Israel—certainly an odd bird for a secular, liberal, intellectual European—but had never actually met an Israeli before. He had also always wanted to learn about Judaism, but had never met a Jew before. To seal our mutual delight at meeting one another, about fifteen minutes into the conversation, he said, "You know, my last name is considered to be a Converso surname."

This so-called Christian shall henceforth be known as Josep. This is not his real name.

How It All Began

Over the next few days, it became apparent that the Powers That Be had not, in fact, provided for my religious needs. There were no kosher meals available, and I shared the room at the hostel with six girls and two guys. Of course, I wasn't going to sleep on the street, so I had to make do; but when it came to food, I was stuck with raw vegetables and the crackers and instant noodle soups I had brought with me. I tried to locate the list indicating what items at the grocery stores were kosher, but failed. I do not remember why, but somehow I didn't make it to the kosher store on Thursday, and on Friday morning I found myself facing an entire Sabbath—usually celebrated with two large, festive meals—with nothing but a bottle of grape juice, a loaf of so-healthy-it-tastes-like-cardboard vegan bread, and a carton of Ben & Jerry's chocolate chip cookie dough ice cream (imported from the USA, of course, where it is certified kosher).

I went to the synagogue that evening to peddle myself as a needy Sabbath guest—a valuable commodity in any self-respecting Jewish community, apart from the one in Barcelona, apparently. The only woman with whom I managed to make enough eye contact to start a conversation turned out to be an American tourist herself, who would have gladly invited me if she didn't have limited rations for herself and her husband. I left the synagogue, defeated, to eat my ice cream.

When Josep learned of my plight, he was appalled. "There has to be a kosher restaurant somewhere," he insisted, and went off on a crusade, if you'll pardon the expression, to find me kosher food. He searched on Google and in the Yellow Pages, and called a bunch of friends. I told him it was hopeless and that I'd done the research, but he would hear none of it. At lunch that day, while I picked at my sliced cucumbers, he asked me, "What if we went to my house and I bought kosher ingredients and cooked for you?"

I looked over at this person who had literally just offered to bring home a random girl from another country, whom he had known for a grand total of seventy-two hours, and cook

her a meal. I shook my head. "No... all the pots and pans would have to be kosher..."
"What if I bought a new pan?"
He couldn't be serious. "It's very nice of you to offer... but it's not just the pans... it's all the utensils and the oven and everything..."
"Is there a way to make them kosher?" he insisted.
I smiled ironically. "Uh... yeah... but trust me, that's not going to happen."
"Why not? What would I need to do?"
"Just trust me. You don't wanna know."
"Tell me. I want to know."
I eyed him skeptically, eyebrows raised. "You really want to know?"
"Yes."
I shrugged. "Okay... *you* asked." Thereupon I launched into a long, rambling explanation of how one kashers a kitchen, which, for the uninformed among you, is a long, painstaking, arduous process that involves a lot of scrubbing, boiling water, and otherwise heat-treating everything. The goal of this tirade was to illustrate just how crazy an idea this was, and I assumed that, after a few sentences, his eyes would glaze over in boredom and that would be that. As predicted, everyone else who had been listening quickly lost interest and began chatting among themselves as I rambled on. But when I glanced at him somewhere in the middle of expounding upon mugs and soapy water in the microwave, he was still watching me as though I were giving him a thrilling play-by-play of the latest Barcelona vs. Madrid soccer game. I skidded to a stop and exclaimed, "Why are you still even *listening* to me?"

To this day, he claims that he couldn't do it only because it was not his own kitchen, and that, if and when I came back to Barcelona, he would, in fact, kasher his kitchen. To this day, *I* claim that he's nuts.

Ironically, it was someone else who managed to locate a restaurant that was "kosher enough"—a vegan restaurant run by a Moroccan Israeli that had at least had kosher certification up until a few months before. I figured that, under the circumstances, this would be acceptable, and we all enjoyed a wonderful meal there. Josep took a seat next to me, and during that conversation, it became clear to me that he was interested in researching his possibly Jewish heritage and learning more about my faith. We parted that night, promising to stay in touch.

And so began an enthusiastic correspondence through which a deep friendship emerged. The combination of my passion for both writing and Judaism, and such an appreciative audience, resulted in my writing long, rambling e-mails explaining Jewish concepts, holidays, and traditions. Our correspondence slowed and then almost petered out over the years, until October of 2013, when I received a message from him out of the blue that he was finally coming to Israel. In November, I finally got to accompany him in person to the Western Wall. Despite not having seen each other or spoken to one another in seven years, the expanses of time, space, language, culture, and religion that stretched between us felt like nothing, and I was determined to renew our correspondence. After a while, though, Josep was unable to keep up with it because of some challenging circumstances in his life at the time.

In December, 2014, I had an idea to start a blog, where I could write and post the letters whenever I felt like it, and he could visit and read whenever he was able. I called the blog *Letters to Josep*.

Now, I bring a selection of those letters to you, adapted for print.

I hope you find them entertaining and informative.

Observant Jewish Life

The Basics

JOSEP AND I began our correspondence when he already had a basic idea of some of the major concepts, and having already witnessed a little of what my life was like as an observant Jew. So before we start, let's all get on the same page. An observant Jew is a person of the Jewish nation and faith[3] who observes the Torah and its 613 commandments as interpreted by rabbinic tradition. This body of Jewish law is called *halakha*. The term "observant" is basically interchangeable with the term "Orthodox," but I'm not too fond of that term.[4]

In a nutshell, the observant Jewish lifestyle includes the following:

- Following strict dietary laws, known as "kashrut" (see: *Jew Food*, Parts I, II, and III.)
- Refraining from all acts of creation on the Sabbath (see: *Shabbat: A Sacred Space in Time*.)
- Observing the laws of family purity (see: *Mikveh: A Spiritual Womb*) and appropriate conduct between the sexes.

---

[3] Judaism is unique among the world's religions in that it is not only a religion, it is also a nationality/ethnicity and arguably a race.
[4] See: *Different Kinds of Jews, Part II*.

The Basics

- Observing the Jewish holidays according to Biblical and/or rabbinic tradition (see: *The Jewish Year*.)
- Regular engagement with God and His law through prayer and study (see: *Prayer*, Parts I and II.)
- Other observances as listed in the Torah, too numerous to list here.

What this means practically will be described in detail in the pages to come.
Got it?
No? What is this Torah thing I'm talking about?
Great question. But before we begin...

A Word on Pronunciation

The language Jews use most often during prayers or studying Torah is the language of the Torah itself: Hebrew. The Talmud is written mostly in Aramaic, which is a related language that was spoken in Babylonia when the Talmud was written. Because Hebrew and Aramaic have sounds that do not appear in the English language, sometimes spelling and pronunciation can get confusing. Is it Chanukah, Hanukah, or Hanukkah? All three are correct; "*ch*" is often used to represent the guttural sound of the letter ח (as in the German "Bach" or Scottish "loch"). But there are actually two letters in Hebrew that make this sound: ח and כ. Originally, the sound of the ח was deeper and more guttural than the כ, but in Yiddish and in modern Hebrew, they are indistinguishable.

Nonetheless, being the linguistic nerd that I am, for the purposes of this book I'm going to use two different spellings to represent those sounds. The sound of the ח will be represented by "*ch*," and the sound of the כ will be represented by "*kh*." The exception will be the word "Hassidic," since that is its standard English spelling.

An Introduction to the World's Biggest Book Club

Dear Josep,

Most people who know the basics about Judaism know that our holy book is what we call the Torah. But there is a lot of confusion around this because we have a lot of holy books! The Bible, the Talmud, prayer books, and a whole slew of rabbinic literature from throughout the centuries.

So, in this letter, we're going to make some order in this chaos.

The Torah

This is kind of confusing because the word "Torah" is used to refer to a few different things. It literally means "instruction," and for the most part, when we use it, we're referring to the entire body of teachings and Jewish law, starting with the Bible, and all the way down to the rabbinic literature being written at this very moment. When we say that we believe God gave us the Torah at Sinai, what we mean is that He gave us the Written Torah (which is the first five books of the Bible), and also an Oral Torah, which is meant to be taught from teacher to student and father to son. We'll elaborate more on the Oral Torah later.

An Introduction to the World's Biggest Book Club

As I have mentioned, though, sometimes the word "Torah" refers to the first five books of the Bible: Genesis, Exodus, Leviticus, Numbers, and Deuteronomy. This is also called "the Chumash," which translates well as "the Pentateuch." The Torah was first written down as scrolls. During the beginning of the Second Jewish Commonwealth in Judea, the leaders of the reestablished Jewish community, Ezra and Nehemiah, established a law that the Torah scroll should be read publicly three times a week. They divided the Torah into weekly portions for this purpose. They did this because Jews at the time were poorly versed in Torah and were forgetting how to speak Hebrew. (They spoke Aramaic.) That custom stuck and is still practiced in every observant Jewish community today. The weekly portion is read from the Torah scroll on Mondays, Thursdays, and Shabbat, during prayer services.

Ashkenazi scrolls are generally wrapped around two handles, and covered with a decorative cloth when not in use.

Sephardi scrolls are kept in a special case of wood or metal, wrapped around rods that are turned while the scroll is still in the case.

The scrolls are handwritten on parchment. They must be written by a *sofer stam*, a scribe who has learned how to write using the special calligraphy we use for holy texts—that is, the Torah, *mezuzah* scrolls, *tefillin* scrolls, and the Scroll of Esther (mentioned below). The letters on all these items must be perfect, otherwise they are not fit for use.

If you visit a synagogue during Torah reading or watch a video of it, you will notice that the reader is chanting the words of the Torah in a kind of singing way. This is called "cantillating." There is a very specific system of notes designated for this purpose, which is marked in the Chumash when it is in book form. In scroll form, it does not have any punctuation or marking.

The Tanakh

The word Tanakh is a Hebrew acronym for the words Torah, Nevi'im (Prophets), and Ketuvim (Writings), which essentially make up the Jewish Bible, or, as y'all prefer to call it, the Old Testament. This is the hardcover book I gave you the second time we met.

I should mention here the other important scroll in Jewish life: Megillat Esther, the Scroll of Esther, often referred to as simply "the Megillah." It appears in Writings, and is read from the scroll during the holiday of Purim.

The Talmud

So remember this Oral Torah I mentioned that was supposed to be passed orally from teacher to student? The reason we needed it was that we needed a system to interpret the Written Torah. There are places in the Torah where God says, "Do X as I have described to you," and there is no description in the text. That refers to this Oral Law. In fact, there is a law that we are not supposed to write down the Oral Law, because it is meant to be a "living Torah" that is dynamic and shifts with the new needs and issues of each generation.

But, there was a problem. After the destruction of the Second Temple, the great Torah scholars were being killed and teaching Torah was illegal under the Romans. Under these circumstances, Rabbi Judah the Prince, an important figure at the time, decided that the Oral Torah must be written down to preserve it for future generations. He compiled the teachings into a volume that was completed around the year 200. This book was called the Mishna (which means "teaching").

Another volume was eventually compiled of analysis and commentary on the Mishna, and this was called the Gemara (which means "study" in Aramaic). These two volumes together, the Mishna and the Gemara, comprise the Talmud (which means "study" in Hebrew).

An Introduction to the World's Biggest Book Club

There are two versions of Gemara; one was compiled in Israel and completed around 350-400. This is called the Talmud Yerushalmi—the Jerusalem Talmud. Another was compiled in Babylonia, where the biggest and most important Jewish community was at the time, and it is called the Talmud Bavli (the Babylonian Talmud). The latter is the one most widely studied. It is also much longer and more comprehensive.

The rest of rabbinic literature is basically analysis and interpretation of the Talmud. Except...

The Siddur

The *siddur* (which means "order") is the Jewish prayer book, which you have seen yourself at least twice.

It has been compiled over a long period. Formal prayer was institutionalized by Ezra and Nehemiah for the same reasons mentioned above—mostly to preserve the Jews' Hebrew.[5]

The High Holiday prayers are so different and long that we have a separate book or books for that, called the *machzor* (which means "cycle," referring to the annual cycle of the holidays).

It is also very common to find a book of psalms on the shelf or in the pocket of an observant Jew. It's part of the Tanakh (in Writings), a collection of poem-prayers traditionally attributed to King David.

The Haggadah

The Haggadah (which means "telling" in Hebrew) is a book exclusively read on the first night of Passover during the Seder (the Passover ceremonial meal; see *Passover, Part II: Seder Night 101*). It was compiled during the Mishnaic and Tal-

---

[5] More about the Jewish prayer book in *Prayer, Part II*.

mudic periods, and the text has remained the same for hundreds and hundreds of years. There are a number of precious ancient Haggadot that were created hundreds of years ago and still have the same text we use today.

Turns out, we are known as the People of the Book for a reason...

Love,
Daniella

An Introduction to the World's Biggest Book Club

Shabbat:
A Sacred Space in Time

Dear Josep,

So, Shabbat is something you're a little familiar with, having seen it—or at least part of it—firsthand. But I don't think I've ever really explained it top-to-bottom, and, given its centrality in observant Jewish life, I believe a proper letter is in order.

First of all, as you know, the commandment to "observe the Sabbath day and keep it holy" is not only a Biblical commandment, it is one of the Ten Commandments. There are two reasons listed in the Bible for keeping the Sabbath: "as a remembrance of the Act of Creation," and "as a remembrance of the Exodus from Egypt." That first reason has a fairly straightforward connection to the concept of a day of rest. In Genesis, it says that God created the world in six days and then rested on the seventh. Of course, in the mainstream Jewish interpretation, we don't take any of that literally. For one thing, how could there be "days" before the sun itself was created (on the fourth day)? For another, how could a God, who has no body or needs of any sort, "rest"? What does that even mean? Did He continue creating afterwards? Not that we know of, right? So why do we say He "rested" on the seventh day—what about the eighth, and the ninth, and every day after that?

Shabbat

We must conclude that we're not talking about the kicking-up-your-heels-with-a-glass-of-lemonade-on-a-Sunday-morning kind of rest. And that's good, because if what we're supposed to do on Shabbat is "rest," why aren't we allowed to do something ridiculously easy like flip a light switch, or something relaxing, like playing music?

So here's the thing. In Judaism (and in most spiritual practices) we believe that the physical world that we see, touch, smell, hear, and taste, is just one aspect of the universe, and that there is a parallel spiritual world as well. One of the central concepts of Judaism is channeling the sanctity of the spiritual world into the physical world. We do this through observing the Torah—God's "guide book to life"—which, practically speaking, means observing the commandments. So in a way, the act of keeping a *mitzvah* is a space in the realm of action where the Divine and the mundane interact.

There are a number of "meeting points" between the spiritual and physical worlds according to Judaism. In the realm of space, for example, there is a physical place where the Divine and the mundane meet. That place is—was—the Temple, and by extension, the city of Jerusalem, and the Land of Israel.[6] Their holiness is in that they have a central role in channeling the spiritual into the physical.

There also exists a "meeting point" in the realm of time. That meeting point is Shabbat.

To Jews, Shabbat is a time above time. It exists on a different plane than the rest of the week. The rest of the week, we have a mission in the world: to act as partners in God's creation, to take the raw materials He has given us and build the world into a better place. You know how in the story of man's creation in Genesis, it says that man was created "in God's image." Christians take that in an entirely different direction... but in Judaism, what we believe this means is that God made

---

[6] For more information on the Temple and Jerusalem, see: *Why Jerusalem Matters*.

us like Him by giving us the ability to create. While other animals also have a limited capacity to create things, they do not do so with the intention of creating something new, but rather to sustain themselves. We have an aspiration to become greater than we are and make the world greater than it is. This is what defines us, and this, we believe, is why we are here.

On Shabbat, something changes. We step back from our role as creators, and recognize that we are also a creation. God's creation. If you will, it's sort of like an office party where we toast the Boss to acknowledge His role in making this all possible. So all the things we are prohibited from doing on Shabbat are acts of creation. We are supposed to use that time to focus on everything God gave us and helped us create: family, friends, good food and wine, studying Torah, and otherwise basking in the Divine light. In our tradition, Shabbat is "a taste of the World to Come," in the sense of both the Messianic era, and our idea of Heaven, a time when we will no longer have to partner with God in creation; when our work will be complete, so we can finally rest and enjoy being creations of God.

So what, practically, does this look like? Well, you've seen part of it, but to be comprehensive I'll take us chronologically from lighting the candles to the *Havdalah* ceremony.

Bringing in Shabbat

I will elaborate on the significance of the Shabbat candles in *A Nation of Pyromaniacs*, so I won't get into that here. The lady of the household is usually the one who performs that ritual. We wave our hands in front of the flames in a beckoning gesture, three times, to signify "bringing in" Shabbat, and then we cover our eyes and make the blessing: *"Blessed are You, Lord, our God, King of the Universe, who sanctified us with His commandments and commanded us to light the Sabbath candles."* It is customary for the woman to then pray for her family and herself, as this is considered an auspicious time for prayer.

Shabbat

Then evening prayers are held at the synagogue. I should note, by the way, that morning, afternoon, and evening prayers are not only held at the synagogue on Shabbat, but every day. Men are obligated to pray three times a day in a *minyan*, a quorum of ten men. The Sabbath prayers are longer and more festive. The synagogue we took you to holds prayers in the style of Rabbi Shlomo Carlebach, which means that it has a lot more singing and dancing than most services. In any case, the regular evening prayers are preceded by a collection of psalms and special songs. This section of prayers is called *Kabbalat Shabbat*, "the reception of Shabbat." The most famous of these songs is *Lekhah Dodi*, a poem written by Rabbi Shlomo Alkabetz, a Sephardi Kabbalist who lived in Safed in the 16th century. It is a really beautiful poem that compares the Sabbath to a bride coming to meet her groom (the nation of Israel). The melodies you heard were ones composed by Rabbi Carlebach, but I thought you'd be interested to know about the melody sung in most Sephardi synagogues. It is an ancient Moorish melody brought to Israel by refugees from Spain, so it is actually older than *Lekhah Dodi* itself.[7]

The Evening Feast

After we come home from synagogue, as you know, it's time to eat! We're required to eat three festive meals on Shabbat: one at night, one in the morning/afternoon following prayers, and one toward sunset. The meal opens with the *Kiddush* ceremony, a prayer recited over a goblet of wine. Kiddush means "sanctification," and reciting this prayer over wine is sort of a declaration of the holiness of the day. Why over wine? Because the presence of wine and bread are required for any meal of distinction—a *se'udah*, or feast, which is often required as part of fulfilling a major commandment. We are also

---

[7] There's a wonderful modern rendition by Ehud Banai in his album *Shir Chadash* (NMC, 2008). Google it!

required to have a se'udah following a marriage or a circumcision ceremony. Any significant moment in Jewish life is celebrated with a feast. Which brings me back to what I've been telling you about Jews all these years... we're all about the food!

So the head of the household makes Kiddush and all those present answer, "Amen," and have a sip. Next we must wash for bread. We wash our hands before eating bread all the time; this is not a special Shabbat thing. Like I showed you, we pour water from a cup over our hands, three times for each hand, and then recite a blessing over washing hands. Because washing hands is supposed to occur right before eating bread, we are careful not to speak (except for the blessings and "amen") until we have eaten it, so there is no *hefsek*, or "break," between washing and eating. And that is where my beautiful challahs come in! It is not, of course, required that they be homebaked. I just happen to love baking them. It is also not required that they be braided, or sweet like mine (though that's the Ashkenazi custom). What *is* required is to use two full loaves of bread to make the blessing. They symbolize the manna God gave the Israelites in the desert; every day, each Israelite would get one portion of manna, but on Friday, they would get two, one for Friday and one for Shabbat.

So the head of the household makes the blessing over the challah and then distributes it to the family and guests, and then we are free to proceed with our meal. Beyond the wine and bread, there is no specific requirement for what the meal should contain, though it's customary to serve meat, as it is festive. It's customary to sing special songs about the Sabbath during the meal, and to discuss ideas from the Torah.

Speaking of guests, hosting guests is actually a mitzvah, and it's common to invite friends, neighbors, and family over to share the meals on Shabbat and holidays. It's like a dinner party every single week!

Shabbat Day

In the morning, there are services at the synagogue, during which the weekly portion of the Torah is publicly read. After the service, we have the second feast. In American congregations, it is common to have the Kiddush at the synagogue with wine and refreshments, and then to continue the meal at home starting from the challah. Israelis tend to have prayers earlier and go straight home for Kiddush and the meal. The afternoon is spent enjoying friends and family, reading, napping, and/or studying Torah. There is a specific mitzvah to enjoy oneself on Shabbat, so we try to set aside the best food and (permitted) entertainment for that day.

Se'udah Shlisheet and Havdalah

Toward evening, there are afternoon prayers, and then the third meal: *se'udah shlisheet*. This meal does not require wine or whole loaves of bread, and, in a pinch, it doesn't even have to include bread, so naturally it's a lighter meal. We usually just have more challah with spreads. It's customary to sing songs with sort of sad melodies during this meal, to express our sadness that Shabbat will soon be leaving.

When three stars have emerged, it is time to pray the evening prayers, and then to perform the Havdalah ceremony. Havdalah means "differentiation," and the ceremony marks the end of Shabbat and the beginning of the new week. It is recited over yet another goblet of wine, starting with some verses from Isaiah—*"Here is the Lord of my salvation, I shall trust and I shall not fear; for God is my strength and Divine song, He has become my salvation..."*—and some other verses from the Tanakh. Then, the blessing is made over the wine.

Next comes the blessing for *besamim*. Besamim means "spices." We smell something pleasant, like cloves or cinnamon, to sort of "ease the sadness" of Shabbat leaving. Next comes the blessing over the Havdalah candle.[8] It would be improper to recite a blessing for something and then not use it, so we use the light of the candle to examine our fingernails.

No, this is not because we're bored teenage girls. It's because our nails are the only reflective surface on our bodies, and with the flame representing the Divine, we're meant to reflect that light, like the moon reflects the sun.

Next comes the final blessing: *"Blessed are You, Lord, our God, King of the Universe, who differentiates between holy and mundane, between light and darkness, between Israel and the nations, between the Seventh Day and the Six Days of Action. Blessed are You, Lord, who differentiates between holy and mundane."*

The candle is then put out, usually by spilling a little wine onto a plate and putting the flame out with it. And that's it—the new week has begun! We sing a song asking for God's blessing for the coming week, and for Elijah the prophet to come and announce the coming of the Messiah.

... And then, to clean up the mess!

Thirty-Nine Categories

So now I'd like to elaborate a little more on the restrictions of the Sabbath.

Earlier I said that the kinds of actions that are prohibited are "acts of creation." But what does that mean exactly? How do we know which acts are forbidden, and which are permitted?

The Oral Law teaches that the Divine commandment to avoid acts of creation on the Sabbath was placed, in the Torah, in close proximity to the instructions for building the Tabernacle,[9] to teach that it is precisely the acts of creation used to build the Tabernacle that are prohibited on Shabbat. The Sages identify thirty-nine categories of work that are included. I'm not going to list all of them here, because it will probably

---

[8] For more on the Havdalah candle see: *A Nation of Pyromaniacs*.
[9] The what? See *Why Jerusalem Matters*.

bore you (though, seriously, I never know with you!) and there are plenty of excellent books on the topic. The categories include things like: all kinds of field work and food preparation, slaughtering animals and making material from their skins, building, writing, sewing, etc.

So the thing about these categories is that it's not just the specific action that's prohibited. The category is a sort of template from which we derive all the other actions that are forbidden on Shabbat. So let's take, for example, the category of "smoothing." The original, specific action this refers to is the act of scraping and smoothing an animal skin to use as leather. But what this means as a category, is any action—grinding, scraping, rubbing, polishing, waxing, etc.—that makes any surface smooth. From this, we derive that we're not allowed to spread thick creams on surfaces... including our own skin. So we're not allowed to spread cream on our skin, such as moisturizing lotion or other types of cosmetics. Scraping an animal skin to smooth it may not seem anything like rubbing lotion on one's hands; but the former is a category, and the latter an action that falls under that category.

But that's not all. The Sages also prescribed some additional restrictions for the Sabbath to prevent one from coming close to violating a Torah prohibition, or to preserve the general atmosphere of Shabbat. The most common example is the concept of *muktzeh*. An item that is muktzeh is one that has no permitted use on the Sabbath, such as a pen (which we're not allowed to write with), or a hammer (which we're not allowed to build with). The Torah prohibits the use of these items; the Sages further prohibited carrying or moving these items at all. This process of creating additional restrictions around the original restriction, we call "building a fence around the Torah." It is of utmost importance to us that we completely avoid violating the Law, and we would rather be too careful than accidentally violate something.

This is, of course, just the tip of the iceberg. The restrictions of the Sabbath are extremely numerous and complex. They fill many books, and can take years of intensive study to completely master on an intellectual level. (And the people who do so are called rabbis!) On a practical level, it can take a long time of practicing and studying to observe the Sabbath properly, and even then, many people—even people like me who have been keeping Shabbat since early childhood—inadvertently violate some of the rules. The idea of "building a fence" is to make it as unlikely as possible that those who are not educated on the details of each prohibition will violate a Torah prohibition, even if they inadvertently violate rabbinic ones.

How a Thousand 'Don'ts' Make One Big 'Do'

There's a reason I chose to elaborate on the restrictions of the Sabbath *after* describing the actual experience of celebrating Shabbat: because when you sit down and read a book about the laws of Shabbat, all you will see is "don't do this" and "don't do that" and "this is forbidden" and "one should avoid this"—hundreds and hundreds of "don'ts." That makes it seem like a suffocating day of constant discipline and restraint, trying to avoid forbidden actions. *But that is a severe misrepresentation of what Shabbat is and how we experience it.* Shabbat is not about the "don'ts." It's about the one big "do" that becomes possible because of those "don'ts." The restrictions build a rigid framework—and it is that framework that makes it possible to create that unique environment of spirituality, love, rest, and closeness to God and to family and friends. Sometimes discipline is what gives us our greatest freedom.

Love,
Daniella

Shabbat

Jew Food, Part I:
Vegetarians, Avert Your Eyes

Dear Josep,
   One of the very first topics we discussed to do with Judaism was *kashrut*. As I described in the story of how we met: "I launched into a long, rambling explanation of how one kashers a kitchen, which, for the uninformed among you, is a long, painstaking, arduous process that involves a lot of scrubbing, boiling water, and otherwise heat-treating everything. The goal of this tirade was to illustrate just how crazy an idea this was, and I assumed that after a few sentences [Josep's] eyes would glaze over in boredom and that would be that. As predicted, everyone else who had been listening quickly lost interest and began chatting among themselves as I rambled on. But when I glanced at [Josep] somewhere in the middle of expounding upon mugs and soapy water in the microwave, he was still watching me as though I were giving him a thrilling play-by-play of the latest Barcelona vs. Madrid soccer game. I skidded to a stop and exclaimed, 'Why are you still even *listening* to me?'"
   For reasons I still cannot fathom, you are *still* listening to me, and I think it is high time I gave you a proper explanation of this whole crazy business called kashrut. Or, in the immortal words of the guy at the supermarket in Barcelona upon being asked where the kosher section was: "Jew food."

This is such a broad topic that we're not going to cover it in one letter. We're going to start with a general overview and then go into detail about animal products. In Part II, we'll talk about the various issues involving fruits, veggies, and grains, and in Part III we will talk about the nitty-gritty details, like how to make kosher vessels or dishes non-kosher, and vice versa, as a somewhat more organized recap of that rambling speech I gave you eight years ago. So:

What Is Kashrut?

Kashrut is the observance of the dietary laws of Judaism. The adjective is "kosher," and these words come from the Hebrew root כ.ש.ר., k.sh.r., meaning "proper," "fit," "appropriate." "Non-kosher" is also known in Yiddish as *treif*, from the word *treifa* in Hebrew, which means "carrion."

The rules of kashrut are derived from the Torah, and it is one of the very basic commandments that—along with Shabbat observance—draws the line between observant Jews and non-observant Jews.

There is no reason given in the Torah for why these laws must be observed. Many Sages have tried to explain it in various ways, but ultimately, this is what we call a *chok*—the type of commandment that has no known reason. In other words, a "Because I Said So" commandment. We observe it out of loyalty to God and the belief that there is Divine reason behind it, even if we humans don't or can't comprehend it.

For a practice with no obvious explanation, it is fairly remarkable how strongly kashrut has held within the Jewish community. Many people who don't consider themselves religious make some effort toward kashrut, such as avoiding pork and shellfish. As you know, many of the practices that survived in families of crypto-Jews were practices to do with kashrut—checking eggs for blood, separating milk and meat, separating the fat from the meat, etc. This is testimony to the deep importance and significance of this mitzvah.

At its most basic, kashrut involves:

1) Eating meat, milk, or eggs produced only by **animals that are designated as kosher**, and then, only if they are slaughtered in a certain way;
2) Not eating **forbidden parts of animals** (namely: blood, certain parts of fat, the sciatic nerve, or a limb severed from a live animal);
3) Complete **separation of dairy products and meat products**;
4) Eating only produce that has been grown and harvested in accordance with the **agricultural laws** (if the land is in Israel and owned by a Jew; otherwise, those laws don't apply) and the laws regarding **tithing** (separating portions to give to the poor, and in the days of the Temple, to the Cohanim and the Levites), and that has been properly **checked for insects** (as per item #1);
5) Other "fences" put in place by the rabbis to prevent various issues or commemorate practices that are no longer observed without the Temple, which we will get into as they come up.

This may sound simple enough, but if you're really committed to keeping these laws to the letter, some difficult questions are going to come up. For example: How do we eat meat, but not the blood, especially in an organ such as the liver, which is completely saturated with blood? Is it okay to eat a piece of kosher meat that was cooked together with a piece of non-kosher meat? How many measures must we take to make sure our food is bug-free before resigning ourselves to the fact that we aren't going to catch everything? What counts as "meat" anyway, in terms of separating it from dairy? Does poultry count? What about fish?

And this, my friend, is why a huge chunk of rabbinic literature is devoted to answering these questions and setting down the principles by which we can answer further questions. And this is also why we need rabbis. Rabbis are basically experts in Jewish law. Because you can't expect your average Joe (-seph?)

Jew Food, Part I

to know all the details of these laws, you have these experts in every community who have studied the laws thoroughly and can answer questions that arise on a day to day basis. That is the main function of the observant rabbi.

So, let's get to it:

Which Animals Are Kosher?

Mammals

Most people know that Jews can't eat pork. Pigs are one of the animals listed explicitly in the Torah as not being kosher. But the pig is actually the last in a list of four animals that are mentioned explicitly, the other three being the camel, the rock-badger (also called the hyrax), and the hare. All other mammals are ruled non-kosher if they do not meet the following two criteria: kosher mammals must have cloven hooves, and they must chew their cud.

Chew their what?

Right. So, there are certain herbivores that have a curious way of digesting food. Plants are pretty hard to digest because of all the fiber. So these animals have multiple stomachs, and the food gets swallowed, brought up again, and chewed multiple times before it is fully digested. This multi-chewing process is called "chewing cud."

Practically speaking, this means that cows, sheep, goats, and deer are kosher. (So are giraffes. There's an urban myth that the reason we can't eat them is that their necks are so long we don't know where to cut it to slaughter them in the kosher manner, but that isn't true. We don't eat them for the same reasons everyone else doesn't.) Pigs are specifically mentioned as non-kosher because, while they do have split hooves, they don't chew their cud. Camels, hares, and rock-badgers chew their cud, but their hooves are not split.

39

Birds

In principle, kosher fowl do not have "criteria." There is a list in the Torah (Leviticus 13-20) of birds that are not kosher, and all others are assumed to be kosher. The problem is that, over time, the names referring to specific birds have been forgotten, so we aren't sure what some of them are. The Sages came up with a number of criteria that kosher birds seem to have in common, such as the structure of the foot and the presence of a crop (a little pocket of skin for storing food before it enters the stomach) etc. One obvious thing that kosher birds have in common is that none of them are birds of prey.

Kosher birds commonly eaten are: chicken, turkey, goose, and duck. Quail, pigeons, doves, and swans are also kosher.

Seafood

Kosher seafood is once again identified by two criteria: it must have fins and scales. So, commonly eaten fish like salmon, tuna, carp, mackerel, sardines, perch, etc., are fine. Exotic fish like swordfish and sharks are not (they don't have scales), and neither are shellfish of any kind (no shrimp, lobster, or crab).[10]

Speaking of which...

Creepy Crawlies

In our Western world this makes us all go "Uugghh," and indeed, most bugs, worms, etc. are not kosher. Frogs, snakes, and lizards are also included in this category (*shratzim* is the term for creatures that creep on the ground). But, there are certain kinds of locusts that are kosher. I am told they are a delicacy in some parts of the world.

I am not sold.

---

[10] Okay, but seriously, with all due respect, *what* is appetizing about those marine cockroaches exactly?!

Kosher Slaughter: Shechita

Very simply, kosher animals must be slaughtered by having their throats slit quickly, with a very sharp knife, in a way that strikes major blood vessels leading to the brain, causing immediate and irreversible loss of consciousness. This must be done very precisely so as to cause minimal suffering to the animal, and therefore *shechita* is a craft that must be studied carefully. The purpose, obviously, is to slaughter the animal in a way that is as humane as possible. A certified Jewish ritual slaughterer is called a *shochet*.

Preparing Kosher Meat

So, once the animal is dead, the blood of the animal must be covered with earth, and then the blood must be removed from the meat. This is done through a process of salting, which is where kosher salt got its name. A more accurate name would be koshering salt, as its purpose is to kasher (i.e. make kosher) the meat. All salt is kosher.

I'm told that kosher meat is thus drier and saltier than non-kosher meat.

As to our question about liver before, salting is not enough to remove the blood from liver, and therefore liver must be broiled in a way that draws out the blood. Other meat can be kashered this way, too.

Milk and Meat

One very common question among newcomers to Judaism—or skeptics—is, however did we get from, "Don't cook a kid in its mother's milk" (Exodus 23:19 and 34:26, and Deuteronomy 14:21), to waiting several hours after consuming any kind of meat, until consuming any kind of dairy? This is one of the prime examples of the importance of the Oral Torah. Through the oral tradition, we know that this phrase refers to all meat and all milk. There are a number of different explanations given for why the Written Torah specifies "kid in its mother's milk," but this is one of the things in the oral tradition that the rabbis are in completely unanimous agreement about, which, as you know, isn't to be taken lightly![11]

The Sages did expand cattle meat to include all other kinds of meat and poultry, but not fish or locusts.

Why do we wait between eating meat and milk? That also has a number of explanations, but for one thing, it demonstrates the severity of this practice and how very careful we are to maintain this complete separation. There are different traditions about how long to wait, ranging from one hour to six hours. We wait three.

That's quite enough for now!

Love,
Daniella

---

[11] Josep and I make constant references to the irrefutable truth behind the joke, "Two Jews, three opinions..."

Jew Food, Part I

Jew Food, Part II:
The Vegetarian Section
(Well, Sort Of)

Dear Josep,

Welcome to Part II of the Great Jew Food Tirade! In this part we're going to talk about plants.

Now, if you can recall what my plate looked like while you and the rest of the press team were happily devouring your delicious meals, you'll remember that fruits and vegetables, as a general rule, are just fine within the laws of kashrut. So why am I writing an entire section on them? Well...

Mitzvot HaTluyot Ba'Aretz
(Commandments Connected
to the Land of Israel)

Observant Jews do, indeed, wander freely through the produce aisles of supermarkets in the USA and Europe. It is actually in the land of Israel that we have to be more careful. While there is no inherent problem with any plant when the land is owned by a Jew and is located in Israel, there are a number of commandments that must be observed for the plants to be okay to eat. These are the *mitzvot hatluyot ba'aretz*.

I am not going to elaborate on what all these commandments are, because there are a lot of them and the details will probably bore you. But they basically split into three categories: commandments that involve giving to the poor (such as leaving fallen grapes or stalks for them to collect, leaving a section at the corner of the field unharvested for them to harvest, etc.), and that are connected to the Temple service (such as: *bikkurim*—bringing the first fruits to the Cohanim at the Temple; *terumah* and *ma'aser*—tithing; and *challah*, probably where the name of the Shabbat bread came from—separating a portion of the bread dough for the Cohanim); or other issues of sanctity, such as the prohibition against crossbreeding plants or eating fruits from a tree in the first three years after it is planted.

Now, the ones connected to the Temple are no longer relevant. Some of them are observed sort of symbolically (like terumah, ma'aser, and challah), but they still must be observed for the produce to be considered kosher. And then there's *shmita*, the observance of the seventh agricultural year, when we are not allowed to work the land as usual, which is a whole other can of worms.[12]

For fields owned by non-Jews or located outside of Israel, these commandments are not relevant.

However, there are other problems associated with products produced in non-Jewish settings...

Wine

So, for instance, you have known for a long time that there is such a thing as kosher wine, by which one would logically (and in this case, correctly) deduce that there is such a thing as non-kosher wine. But think about this for a minute. We're talking about 100% pure crushed grapes, fermented in barrels that hold nothing else. Grapes are inherently kosher, and if the mitzvot hatluyot ba'aretz are not in the picture, what could possibly be non-kosher about wine?

---

[12] A letter specifically about shmita can be found on the blog: letterstojosep.com/shmita

According to the Talmud, there are a number of things that must be avoided under the general prohibition of idolatry. One of them is drinking wine that is used for some kind of ceremonial practice by idolaters.

But, I hear you say, that would explain why you couldn't drink wine made in, say, India. But what about wine made by Christians or Muslims, who are, for the most part, not considered idolaters? ("For the most part," because we have issues with the concept of the Trinity. But the Sages who actually lived among Christians did not consider it idolatry. We have no such debate regarding Islam.)

So, the Sages extended the prohibition to include all non-Jews *and* non-observant Jews, pretty much because you don't really have any way to know what their beliefs about the wine are, and because of the severity of idolatry, we need to be extra, extra careful about this. Idolatry is one of the only three commandments that we are not allowed to transgress even if it means our only other option is to die. The other two are murder and sexual immorality.

Digging through my archives, I discovered that you actually provided another answer to this question when we first discussed this issue many years ago. I told you that our editor-in-chief in Spain had asked why we still observe this law about wine if there is no longer idolatry in the Western world. You said: "I disagree with [her] about the idolatry thing. Maybe we don't have idols like in the old times, but there's still a lot of idolatry with things like the TV, supermodels or superstars, money, fame, sex... And it's caused by the same basic principle: the emptiness of the soul. When you're full of God, you don't need anything more. So you don't have to put the TV at the center of the house, or sex in the center of your life. The old peoples put other gods instead of Him in the center of their lives because they had empty souls. That's what I think."

Well, I'm definitely not arguing with that.

In any case, not so very long ago, you couldn't get really good kosher wines. (Ever heard of Manischewitz? If not, good.) Today, though, there are some really great wineries in

Israel and abroad that produce a wide selection of good kosher wine. Like, for instance, the one you bought us last time you were here, which we finally opened a couple days ago. (And is, by the way, delicious. Thank you.)

Baking and Cooking by Gentiles

Another issue that comes up here is bread that is baked or food that is cooked by a gentile. This is a rabbinic restriction based on the idea that it is difficult to trust someone who does not keep kashrut himself or see any importance in it to be careful enough about it when cooking for you.

There are ways around this. According to Ashkenazi custom, it is enough for a Jew to light the fire for the food to not be considered *bishul nokhri* (food cooked by a non-Jew). That's how kosher restaurants are able to employ non-Jews in the kitchen.

Another restriction I should mention here, even though it concerns an animal product, is *chalav nokhri*. The Sages ruled that we may not consume milk produced by non-Jews (their cattle, that is) out of concern that milks of other, non-kosher animals might be mixed in. The famous American rabbi Moshe Feinstein ruled that this is no longer a concern in places of modern industry where there is strict regulation and supervision, and you can be certain that what you're getting is cow's milk. (This is actually not true in all Western countries, by the way—including Spain. I was told that I couldn't rely on this ruling regarding even plain milk in Spain.) Most Americans hold by this ruling, but many Israelis don't, because of the wide availability of *chalav yisrael* (milk produced by Jews) in Israel. The Rabbinate of Israel holds that derivatives of chalav nokhri (a.k.a. *avkat chalav nokhri*), such as powdered milk, are okay, but not straight milk. So there was a big scandal in recent years about the Rabbinate removing Haagen Dazs ice cream from the shelves, even though it is certified kosher by the Orthodox Union in the USA, because of this difference in halakhic opinion.

Anyway.

In all of the above, beside the practicalities of trusting non-Jews with kashrut... I also see an agenda on the part of the Sages to make it more difficult for Jews to get socially intimate with non-Jews. Jews not being able to eat at non-Jews' tables makes it harder for them to develop the kinds of relationships that could lead to conversion, intermarriage, and assimilation. That may not be so politically correct, but assimilation is the biggest threat to Jewish continuity in the modern era, and... well, this is a topic for a different letter.

Little Friends

So the last issue to do with eating fruits, vegetables, and grains, is the fact that we are not allowed to eat bugs (see Part I) and therefore all edible plants must be thoroughly checked to assure that no creepy crawlies have found their way into our food.

Now, someone who has peeked ahead and knows the $1/60^{th}$ rule that I will explain in the next letter, might ask: unless we're talking about the kind of bug that would make any housewife run screaming, we're talking about tiny, almost microscopic creatures, that are certainly less than $1/60^{th}$ of the volume of the food. So why aren't they *batel* ("nullified")? Because they are a *briya shleima*, a "whole creature." Meaning that, because it's the bug's whole body, it cannot be nullified. But then how do we ever eat anything?! What about microscopic bugs?!

So this rule only applies to bugs that can be seen by the naked eye. If you need a magnifying glass, let alone a microscope, to see it, then it doesn't count.

Still, you can imagine, checking for bugs can be incredibly labor intensive and frustrating. For some kinds of fruits and veggies, it's no big deal—fruits, including fruits that are generally thought of as vegetables (like cucumbers and tomatoes), only require a once-over to make sure they don't have wormholes or something like that. By contrast, leafy green vegetables must be pulled apart, soaked in water with soap or salt or vinegar, and then examined. Leaf. By. Leaf. (I should mention that there are different standards, and some are more lenient—allowing the check of a representative sample, for instance, but checking each leaf individually is the mainstream view.)

One way of getting around this problem is growing the plants in special conditions where bugs are extremely unlikely to come in contact with the vegetables. In Israel, Gush Katif vegetables are grown hydroponically, meaning that they are grown in greenhouses, detached from the soil.

The environment is carefully controlled to assure that no bugs will get in. In this case, we are permitted to eat the produce without checking for bugs (but most authorities still require a thorough soaking and rinsing before use). There is also an opinion that frozen vegetables are not a problem because any bugs that may be in there will explode in the freezing process (!) and therefore are no longer "whole creatures." This is not exactly reassuring, but our bug-free standards are way higher than pretty much anyone else's, and you have to draw the line somewhere...

So that concludes Part II!

Love,
Daniella

Jew Food, Part III:
In Which Things Get
Ridiculously Complicated

Dear Josep,

So, we've covered the issues with animals and animal products, and with plants and their products. None of this has explained why I answered, "No," when you asked me if I could eat something made of kosher ingredients that you cooked in your kitchen, nor why I couldn't simply eat the vegetarian food I was offered at the conference.

The reason for this can be summarized in one halakhic term: *ta'am*, which translates as "flavor."

What does it really mean, the Sages asked themselves, to avoid eating a certain type of food? What in the experience of eating a non-kosher product is prohibited? So the answer in our tradition is that it is the *flavor*—the ta'am—of the non-kosher product, which we must avoid. This principle expresses itself in how we answer questions about the level of separation between non-kosher and kosher food and meat and milk.

The problem, of course, is that if it's the flavor that makes the difference, how are we supposed to make a ruling about something if we can't actually taste it out of concern that it may not be kosher? Sephardim actually hold that you can give the food to a non-Jewish cook (or someone else who is involved in the food industry and has an incentive to give an accurate answer) and rely on his answer about whether the flavor of the non-kosher product is discernible. But for the most part, we rely on the following principles:

K'Bol'o Kakh Polto—
'As It Absorbs, so It Emits'

This is the principle about the utensils we use to cook and eat the food. Halakhically speaking, utensils absorb the flavors of the food cooked or served on it, *as long as the food is hot*. How hot? The Sages say: "*Yad soledet bo.*" Basically, too hot to comfortably touch. Aside from temperature, there is also *harifut*—strength of flavor. Some foods are considered to have particularly strong flavors, such as onions, garlic, and citrus fruits. Those transfer their flavor even without heat.

Practically speaking, this means we have to have two sets of dishes and utensils: one for milk, and one for meat. (We also have a bunch of pots and a big vegetable knife that are *pareve*—neither milk nor meat—so we can make food that can be eaten with either meat or milk.) It also means that we can't use any dish or utensil that has been used to cook non-kosher food, at least with hot food.

It is from this principle—that utensils absorb the flavor and emit the flavor the same way—that we learn how to kasher (i.e. make kosher) utensils. So if I normally use a pot to cook food by boiling it, that means the flavors of that food can be removed by boiling water in the pot. If an oven absorbs flavor by its heat, you need to clean out the oven of any bits of food that might be stuck in it, and then leave it at its highest temperature for an hour or so.

That's the basic idea. Now I know what you're thinking—oh, that sounds easy enough. Have you ever tried scrubbing every last inch of the inside of your oven? Unless you have a self-cleaning mechanism, this is really irritating and difficult work. I know, because we have to do it every year for Passover,

(Just wait 'till I tell you about the restrictions around Passover!) Some things need to be torched (yes, with a blow torch) to burn out the flavor.

It should be noted that modern stainless steel is a lot less porous than the metals that were once used for things like this, so this is very, very strict and probably unnecessarily so. Sephardim hold that because glass is not porous, it cannot absorb flavors and therefore would not need to be kashered. (Unfortunately for me, Ashkenazim do not hold this way.) There is a rabbi in Hebron who, after reviewing a scientific study about the absorption levels in stainless steel, ruled that stainless steel should be considered like glass, but with the caveat that no one should hold this way unless another two prominent rabbis agree with him. As far as I know, this hasn't happened yet.

Ta'am Lifgam (Unpleasant Flavor) and Ben Yomo (of the Same Day)

Another principle is that the ta'am is only a problem if the flavor being transferred is desirable and pleasant. So, for example, if I'm washing dishes with hot water, and I accidentally use the meat sponge instead of the milk one, it's okay because the dish soap gives it an unpleasant flavor.

This principle allows for the principle of *ben yomo*—the idea that after twenty-four hours, a flavor that was absorbed into a utensil is no longer pleasant. So for example, say I have a pot that was used to cook meat within the last twenty-four hours. If I cook dairy in it, even if it was clean, the dairy food is not kosher and the pot needs to be *kashered*. If, however, I cooked meat in it more than twenty-four hours ago, the pot will still need to be *kashered*, but the dairy food is okay to eat, because the flavor it absorbs from the pot is not a pleasant flavor.

Batel B'Shishim (Nullified in Sixty)

Friday morning. Eitan's amazing Shabbat chicken soup is bubbling away on the stove. One of my curious little gremlins, who happens to be munching on a slice of cheese, quietly and stealthily slides the step stool over to the sink, and before I have a chance to stop him—drops a bit of the cheese in the soup!

What do we do?! In my household, Shabbat without a bowl of chicken soup is like a Christmas without El Caga-tío![13] *Can Shabbat be saved?*

The answer is: probably. According to the principle of *batel b'shishim*, the flavor of any given food becomes nullified—batel—when it is mixed with another food that is at least sixty times its volume. So in this case, I'd have to fish out the bit of cheese I could still see if it hadn't melted completely into the soup yet, but as long as it was just a little bit and there was enough soup in the pot, and there is no recognizable cheese in the soup, then it's batel and the soup is fine.

Phew!

Note, however, that this rule does not count for foods that are considered *charif* (spicy or strong-flavored) for obvious reasons. I'm sure you know what one clove of garlic or a squeeze of lemon can do for a dish.

To Summarize

The easiest way to think about this is to think of kashrut as a sort of "spiritual allergy." Someone who has a severe allergy to peanuts or gluten can't eat things that contain even tiny traces of those foods, or that were processed in the same factory or cooked using the same utensils. Kashrut is actually less stringent than this after the fact, but the level of care we take to avoid any "contamination" of non-kosher foods or mixing

---

[13] See *A Little Catalan Context*

Letters to Josep

of meat and milk is on the level of a severe celiac avoiding gluten. (I'm stepping away from the peanut allegory, because there are people who will have an allergic reaction just from sitting in the same room with someone who opens a bag of peanuts... and, as you know, I'm perfectly fine with sitting in the same room as someone eating non-kosher food.)

And the bottom line, of course, is that keeping kosher is hard! I grew up with it, so it comes fairly naturally, but even so, every once in a while I'll reach for the wrong spatula or pour hot food into the wrong mixing bowl. I know enough about the laws of kashrut that I usually know when something is okay, but when I'm not sure or I think it might not be okay, I relay the question to Eitan, whose rabbinical expertise focuses on this topic. Sometimes, though, even he will be stumped and will bump the question up to a higher authority, and give one of his rabbis a call.

This concludes our Great Jew Food Tirade!

Still convinced you're going to kasher your kitchen for me if and when I come visit?! If you are, I clearly haven't done my job! It may require further reading to properly dissuade you. The Chabad website has a comprehensive guide to kashering a kitchen.

But, as I was then, I am very touched by your intentions. I will be perfectly happy with sandwiches on paper plates if the occasion ever does arise.

Lots of love,
Daniella

Jew Food, Part III

Prayer, Part I: Why Pray?

Dear Josep,

So I was going to write a letter about prayer. But then, as often happens, I found out I was writing two letters. The first one is about the concept of prayer in Jewish thought, and the second will be about the formal Jewish prayers and the structure of Jewish prayer services.

We're going to define prayer as the act of speaking to God. In Judaism, we have formal prayers that we are required to recite daily and/or in various situations (blessings, for example). But there is also "spontaneous" prayer: speaking to God whenever you like, asking Him for things you want or need, thanking Him for good things that have happened to you, or generally sharing your thoughts and desires with Him. In Judaism, we divide prayer into three elements: *shevach* (praise); *bakasha* (request); and *hodaya* (thanksgiving). Jewish prayers usually contain all three of these elements, and usually in that order. Spontaneous prayer can be in whatever language you like, but all formal prayers, across the globe, are conducted in Hebrew (or sometimes Aramaic) for reasons we have already discussed.[14] In Judaism, you have to really speak the words to pray. Intention, or thinking the words, is not enough. Even

---

[14] In *An Introduction to the World's Biggest Book Club*.

during "silent" prayers, we must whisper the words to ourselves loud enough so that we can hear ourselves.

But... why talk to God at all? If you think about this a little, it's actually a pretty good question. If we believe that God is Ultimate Good, and that everything that happens in the world—even things that seem terrible—is for the ultimate good of all existence, why bother asking God to intervene? He's going to do what's best for us anyway, isn't He? And doesn't God know our thoughts? Why do I need to verbalize what I want from Him? He's supposed to know already.

To be honest, I still struggle with this question, but my struggle is more personal than theological. It is very difficult for me to ask for something when I know the answer might be negative. And, as you know from knowing me personally, it's very difficult for me to send a question, a request, or a sensitive statement out into the void and get no response. Even *wanting* something I know I might not be able to have can be very painful for me. So putting that desire into words, and offering it up to this invisible, omniscient, omnipresent Being Who will never give me a clear and obvious response, puts me in an extremely vulnerable position. And Judaism—as you will see in Part II—requires us to ask for things we probably can't have *every day*, *several times a day*. Every single day we pray for the redemption and the coming of the Messiah, not just eventually, but *mehera*—speedily, *b'karov, beyamenu*—soon, in our time. And though we're supposed to believe that it's possible that he will come any minute, realistically many of us don't think the world is ready for it yet. There have been times in my life that I simply couldn't say these words anymore. I couldn't say them with intention and really open myself up to wanting God to answer, when I knew that He probably wouldn't. I couldn't take the constant sense of rejection and disappointment, feeling like I was pleading in vain and repeatedly banging on the proverbial gates of Heaven, with no answer.

Well, to address the theological question, we will need... a little Hebrew grammar lesson!

Letters to Josep

The word "to pray" in Hebrew is להתפלל (*lehitpalel*). Hebrew has a number of verbal conjugations that can give the same root different meanings. For instance, using the root נ.ק.ה., you can say לנקות (*lenakot*) meaning "to clean," or להתנקות (*lehitnakot*) meaning "to be cleansed." The latter conjugation is reflexive, meaning that the object and the subject of the verb are the same ("to ___ oneself"), much like one of the uses for the *se* pronoun in Spanish (going with the example above: *lavar* vs. *lavarse*).

The conjugation used in the word להתפלל is reflexive: "to make oneself pray"; *orarse*.

What does this mean?

The idea is that praying is not something you do to God. It is something you do to yourself. It is something that affects, changes, and refines you spiritually. And maybe, in so doing, you can change your part in the situation enough that God will change how He chooses to conduct matters in a way that is easier for you.

Sometimes this is a vague theoretical idea, but sometimes it is very real. How many times have you prayed for strength, only to discover that the very act of praying gave you strength? I don't know about you, but this has happened to me a lot. By elevating myself spiritually, by connecting to God in this very personal and—for me—vulnerable way, sometimes I can make myself worthy of an easier path to wherever He has been leading me. And sometimes, prayer gives me the strength to handle it when God's answer is "No."

In Judaism, we believe that every single prayer makes an impact, but we don't always know what the impact is. Sometimes we're disappointed because He doesn't answer our prayers the way we would have liked. Sometimes it feels like He's not listening. But we believe that He *is* always listening, and He always answers—sometimes with "revealed good," and sometimes with "hidden good" which may look like evil or hardship to us.

Many people have experienced crises of faith because of disasters that happened to them despite their prayers. But seeing God this way is limiting Him. He is not a soda machine where, if you punch in the right code, He'll give you exactly what you asked for. God doesn't always give us what we ask for, but He always gives us what we need. Sometimes what we need is terribly hard and excruciatingly painful. True faith in God is believing that He always gives us what is truly best for us on a cosmic and spiritual level, even if our limited human capacity for understanding cannot fathom the purpose of some things that happen.

There is an idea in Judaism that the strength of one's prayers increases during key moments of joy in their lives, such as on one's wedding day, during childbirth, on a birthday, etc. These moments are also moments of spiritual transformation and renewal. There is also an idea that people who are closer to God spiritually have greater "spiritual power," so their prayers are more likely to be answered; and that when you pray for someone else, your own prayers for yourself are answered first. All these strengthen the idea that it is not the request itself that can make an impact, but the spiritual process happening within the person making the request, and the impact that spiritual change has on the rest of the world.

Prayer is sometimes referred to as *avodah* in Hebrew, which means "work." Sometimes prayer is as easy as telling your son, "I love you." Sometimes, it's as hard as asking someone you have hurt deeply to forgive you. Either way, in the moments that we connect and open ourselves up to Him, we allow Him into our lives, and that helps us grow and inch closer to our potential and our purpose in the world.

May all your prayers be answered with revealed good.

Lots of love,
Daniella

Prayer, Part II:
A Peek into the Jewish Prayer Book

Dear Josep,

In Part I, we discussed the concept of prayer in Jewish thought. Today, we're going to get into the technicalities of formal Jewish prayer.

So first of all: why do we have formal prayer at all? Why not just say whatever we like whenever we like? Well, the first reason is, as I've explained before, to help the Jews maintain a regular use of Hebrew. (As I mentioned, formal prayers are always conducted in Hebrew—with some prayers in Aramaic.) Needing to pray in a group (as I will elaborate later) also forces Jews to live close together, maintaining ties with a community. Having a specific liturgy helps us all focus on the things that are most important to us as individuals and as a nation. I would say the main functions of formal prayer are to connect us with one another as a community, unifying us in our service of God, and to institute connecting with God as a regular practice throughout the day, providing a formula and framework for an "effective conversation" with Him.

When I say "formal prayers," I'm including all the prescribed prayers that you will find in the siddur (or machzor—High Holiday prayer book). Now, if you've ever cracked open a siddur, you'll know that there's no way we'll cover everything that's in there in this one letter. I'll describe the basic structure of the prayers and prayer services, building from the "core" of the prayers outward. Which means, we must start with...

The Amidah

Formal prayers as a daily practice began at the beginning of the Second Temple period, with the composition of the *Amidah* prayer, also known as the *Shmone Esrei*. "Amidah" means "standing," referring to the fact that it is recited while standing. "Shmone Esrei" means "eighteen," because it was originally composed of eighteen blessings (another was added later) addressing a variety of universal topics. Remember how we mentioned that Jewish prayer is usually structured using the praise-request-thanksgiving formula? So the Shmone Esrei begins with praise: praising God for His treatment of us and our forefathers, for His might and kindness, and for His holiness. Next come the request prayers. We pray for knowledge and understanding; for repentance and for God to draw us nearer to His will; for forgiveness; for redemption; for health and healing; for prosperity; for the ingathering of the exiles; for the restoration of justice; for the annihilation of evil and evildoers; for the welfare of the righteous; for the rebuilding of Jerusalem; for the restoration of the Davidic royal dynasty (a.k.a. the Messiah), and, lastly, for God to accept all our prayers. Then comes thanksgiving. We thank God for our lives, for "Your miracles that are with us every day," for "Your wonders and goodness at all times," and His eternal kindness. Finally, we pray for peace and His blessing in all things, and thank Him for blessing us with peace.

During services, this prayer is first recited in silence, every person to him or herself. We recite it while standing with our feet together, which is symbolic of the angels (who are described somewhere as having only one foot) while facing Jerusalem. At the beginning and the end of the prayer, we take three steps backwards, and then three steps forward. There are a number of reasons for this, some of them having to do with the Temple services, but this is how I like to think about it: Before the prayer, we "step back" from the material world and then "step up" before the King of Kings. After the prayer, we back respectfully away from our Master and return to the material world. We also bow during certain parts of the prayer, as though bowing before the King.

After the silent recitation, the *chazzan*—the cantor—repeats the entire prayer out loud. This practice was established for those Jews who couldn't read and couldn't memorize this (rather long) prayer. They can fulfill their duty to pray it by answering "Amen" when the chazzan completes each blessing.

Prayer Services

Jews are required to recite many prayers throughout the day (most of them blessings), but as a general rule there are three prayer services that we are required to attend. (By "we," I mean men. In Orthodox Judaism, women are exempt from the commandments that have specific prescribed times. Women are also required to pray, but not necessarily at the prescribed times and not necessarily three times a day.) The prayer services are *Shacharit* (morning services), *Mincha* (afternoon services), and *Ma'ariv/Aravit* (evening services). They were established in memory of the three daily sacrifices at the Temple that corresponded to them. As a rule, men are supposed to attend these services and pray with at least nine other men (in a *minyan*—a quorum of ten men; in Orthodoxy, women are not counted for this because they have a different "level" of requirement for this particular commandment). In practice, if they can't attend a synagogue for whatever reason, they may pray on their own, but certain prayers that are recited in a minyan must be omitted.

On Mondays, Thursdays, and Shabbat, a weekly portion of the Torah is read during the morning services, after the chazzan's repetition of the Amidah. On Shabbat, *Rosh Chodesh*, and holidays, there is an additional prayer service called Musaf (meaning "addition") that corresponds to an additional sacrifice that was offered on those days. It is usually recited right after morning services, as part of the same service.

Composition of the Services

The morning service can be rather lengthy, lasting thirty to forty-five minutes in a synagogue on a weekday, and longer on Shabbat or a holiday. It begins with a series of "morning blessings," thanking God for basic things like eyesight, clothing, being able to walk, etc. Then, there is a series of psalms and other prayers that fall under the *shevach* (praise) category. Next comes the *Shema* prayer,[15] which is preceded and followed by two long blessings. Then comes the Amidah, and depending on the tradition of the congregation, there may be a number of other psalms and prayers read before the service is concluded with a special prayer called *Aleinu* ("It Is Upon Us") that is about our responsibility to now go out into the world and proclaim God's glory, and the *Kaddish* prayer—a special prayer in Aramaic about God's supremacy and holiness. (I'll get back to it when we talk about Jewish mourning practices, because at certain points in the service, only mourners—those who have lost a close family member in the past year—say this prayer.)

The Mincha service is much shorter, consisting only of a few psalms, the Amidah, and Aleinu. Ma'ariv is also short like this, but it includes reading the Shema again before the Amidah, with slightly different blessings preceding and following it. On Shabbat and holidays, the Amidah is different. It includes only seven blessings, not eighteen, because we don't do request prayers on Shabbat and holidays. Instead, there are different blessings specific to the day. This is also true of Musaf. On Shabbat and holidays there are also additional songs and prayers, and certain prayers that are omitted.

---

[15] See: *On the Doorposts of Your Home: All About Mezuzot.*

Other Prayers

I've written about blessings before,[16] but there are also a few other prayers we say that are not part of the daily prayer service. One of them is the prayer we recite upon waking in the morning, Modeh/Modah ani: "*I give thanks to you, living and eternal King, for returning my soul to me. Great is Your faith.*" That last bit contains a very deep idea—God has returned my soul to me, not because of my faith in Him, but because *He* has great faith in *me*. He returned my soul to me because He trusts that I will contribute goodness to His world and work to fulfill my role here, whatever that may be.

Another prayer worth noting is *tefillat ha'derekh*, the traveler's prayer. It is a short prayer for safety we recite upon leaving the city limits. The roads here being as they are, this is a prayer I recite with particular intention and fervor every time I leave town...

Accoutrements

Generally speaking, no special equipment or attire is required for prayer; one must be at least minimally clothed, of course, and it is proper to be fully dressed, with our heads covered,[17] out of respect for the Guy to Whom You Are Speaking (hence the kippah). However, if you ever stumble across a Jewish man in prayer on a weekday, a rather strange sight will greet your eyes. He will have a little black box tied to the front of his head with a thick leather strap, and another box tied to his arm near the shoulder, with another leather strap winding around the rest of his arm and then around his middle finger.

---

[16] See: *Blessings: Finding God in an Apple*.
[17] *Kippot* is the plural of *kippah*, also known in Yiddish as a *yarmulke*: a special cap that Jewish men wear. Josep knows all about this and owns at least one, which he likes to wear when he visits us and confuse all my neighbors.

He also might be wearing a wool shawl with fringes and two blue stripes over his head.

The shawl is a prayer shawl, a *tallit*, and the boxes are phylacteries, tefillin. The prayer shawl is a four-cornered garment, so it has tassels (*tzitziyot*) at each corner, according to the commandment of *tzitzit* (described in *Links in the Chain: On Educating Children*). The stripes of the tallit inspired the blue stripes on the Israeli flag, symbolizing the State as the culmination of our prayers for two millennia. For the record, that's what's supposed to go in that velvet bag of yours.[18]

Tefillin is a separate commandment, mentioned in the Torah a number of times, one of which is the Shema prayer: "*You shall bind [the words of the Torah] as a sign upon your arm, and they shall be as a reminder between your eyes.*" (Deuteronomy 6:8) So that's what those little black boxes are. They are leather boxes that contain parchment scrolls, on which four passages from the Torah are inscribed—two from Exodus, and two from Deuteronomy, the latter two being the first two paragraphs of the Shema.

The boxes are bound to the body with leather straps: one on the forehead ("between the eyes") and one on the inner side of the arm—the left arm if you're right-handed, and the right if you are left-handed. Men are required to put on tefillin every day except Shabbat and holidays. Women are not required because of the same rule mentioned before. We are also not forbidden to do it, but there's a very strong tradition for women not to, and in the vast majority of Orthodox circles, women don't. I suspect that, very slowly, over the next few decades,

---

[18] Josep sent me some pictures of his room back in November 2006, "to help me get to know him better." After noting, with amusement, the big Israeli flag hanging over the bookshelf, I squinted at one particular spot on his dresser and was like, "Wait... is that a tefillin bag? And a kippah?! What is a non-practicing Roman Catholic in Barcelona doing with those things?!" He explained that they were gifts from a friend who had traveled to Jerusalem, and after some back-and-forth we figured out that the bag said "tallit" on it.

this will change. In Conservative and Reform circles, women do put on tefillin.

The Torah explains that the purpose of tefillin is to serve as a reminder of God's intervention in the Exodus from Egypt. Practically speaking, having a physical object connected to prayer on your body helps channel your concentration and maintain an awareness and focus on God.

On Another Personal Note

I shared in my previous letter that I sometimes struggle with spontaneous request prayer. I really struggle with formal prayer, too—and always have. It's very difficult to maintain *kavana* (intention, concentration, and focus) on the same exact words every single day. I find that it's much easier to connect and feel that the prayer is "doing something for me" when I have a longer space between prayers. Especially with children around, it's really a challenge. I get very frustrated when I'm interrupted, and, as you full well know, there's no way to be around young kids without being interrupted every thirty seconds. So I tend to rely on the most lenient opinion that women are only required to say one prayer per day, and that it doesn't have to be the Amidah—just something structured with the praise-request-thanksgiving formula. I know the idea is perseverance, continuing to "show up" even when you don't feel like it and even when you can't do it as well as you'd like or should. And obviously, that's something I need to keep working on. I hope when my kids get older I'll feel more available to pray regularly. It's strange; it seems like such a burden when I think about it, but on the rare occasions when I actually pick up my siddur and start to pray, it usually feels like a breath of fresh air for my soul.

I will conclude with this section of the Sephardic version of the *Amidah:*

Hear our voice, Lord our God; Merciful Father, have compassion upon us and accept our prayers willingly and with mercy and favor; for You are God who hears prayers and supplications; and from before You, our King, do not turn us away empty-handed. Have mercy on us, and answer us, and hear our prayer. For You hear the prayer of every mouth.
Blessed are You, Lord, Who hears prayer.

Love,
Daniella

Mikveh:
A Spiritual Womb

Dear Josep,

Anybody who knows anything about Jewish archaeology knows that there are three main architectural markers that indicate that a settlement was Jewish. One, of course, is an indentation on the doorpost for the mezuzah. Another, obviously, is the existence of a synagogue. The third is the *mikveh*, the ritual bath. I know you have heard of these because you mentioned the discovery of a ritual bath in the ancient Jewish quarter of Girona.

So what are these baths, what are they used for, and why are they the first structure a Jewish community builds—even before the synagogue?

What Is a Mikveh?

The word "mikveh" (often spelled and pronounced "mikvah" in English, but "mikveh" is a more accurate transliteration) means a "collection" or a "gathering." A mikveh is a collection of water from a natural source. This can be a naturally occurring "collection," such as a spring, lake, sea, or ocean; or, it can be an artificial "collection," but this has to be done in a very specific way to maintain the water's "natural" status. One parameter is that a mikveh must contain at least 750 liters of water (198 gallons).

What Is It Used For?

Well, now that we have no Temple, there are three main uses, which I will describe below. But back in the days of the Temple, immersion in a mikveh was an imperative part of the spiritual purification process required of anyone who visited or worked at the Temple.

What Is Tahara (Ritual Purity)?

Let's get this straight before we go on: The mikveh is indeed a "bath" that uses water, but when we use the concepts of purity (*tahara*) and impurity (*tum'a*), we are **not** talking about cleanliness. Tahara and tum'a are simply different spiritual states of being. Tum'a is a state that is associated with a variety of restrictions, depending on the type of the impurity. We know nothing about what it actually is, or means, but it is often associated with death in some form. Tahara is its opposite. This is a vast subject in Jewish law, most of which is not currently relevant because the Temple does not currently exist, and most of the matters pertaining to ritual purity have to do with Temple service. The only type of tum'a that is currently relevant, and can be reversed by immersion in a mikveh, is *niddah*. We'll get to that in a moment.

A Gateway to Another State of Being

So why is water required for this purification process? There is much to be said about the symbolism and spiritual significance of water, and it is not unique to Judaism. Christianity and Islam also use water for spiritual purification. (The differences between immersion in the mikveh and baptism will become clear over the course of the letter.) In Rabbi

Aryeh Kaplan's book *The Waters of Eden*, he explains that all naturally occurring water in the world originated in the four rivers of the Garden of Eden that are mentioned in Genesis, and thus, natural water sources connect us physically to our spiritual source—the state of spiritual purity in which Adam and Eve existed before their sin. That sin is what brought the possibility of death into existence, and as I said, there is a connection between tum'a and death. So it makes sense that contact with the spiritual "matter" of the Garden of Eden would remove the influence of death from our bodies.

When we immerse in the mikveh, we must remove all physical barriers—dirt, stray hair, etc.—and immerse our entire bodies, so that we are completely surrounded by the water. The water can be likened in this way to amniotic fluid, and the mikveh to a spiritual womb—or grave. It is a gateway to another state of being. Thus encompassed in the water, we are "reborn" into a renewed spiritual state—the state of tahara.

Immersion of Vessels (*Tevilat Keilim*)

One of the uses of *mikvaot* today is the ritual immersion of vessels made of metal or glass that were produced by a non-Jew. The Torah (Numbers 31:21-23) tells us that when we want to use vessels made of various kinds of metals that were previously used by non-Jews to prepare or serve food, we must first immerse them in a mikveh. Our Sages decided that glass must also be immersed because, like metal, it can be melded back together if it is broken. Clay or stone vessels do not require immersion.

Why does the Torah require this? The short answer, as with most things to do with ritual purity, is that we don't know. I like to think of it as a way to physically dedicate a vessel for sacred purposes—feeding my children, cooking kosher food, preparing food to celebrate the holidays, etc.; yet another way to bring awareness of the Divine into the mundane.

This is not to be confused with kashering vessels. Immersion of vessels is a separate mitzvah.

Family Purity (*Taharat HaMishpacha*)

So what is niddah? Niddah is a state of tum'a that is brought on by uterine bleeding which usually involves menstruation or postpartum bleeding. Remember how I said that tum'a is usually connected in some way to death? In the case of menstruation, it's not so much death, as the loss of potential for life. Menstruation and postpartum bleeding are also related to Eve's curse, bringing us back to the connection between tahara and the waters of Eden.

In our day, the practical implication of this state of tum'a is just one thing: "*You shall not come near to revealing the nakedness of a woman in her state of niddah.*" (Leviticus 18:19) Sexual relations, and any act that might lead to them, are forbidden. The Sages unanimously agree that this means any kind of physical contact between a woman in niddah and a man who is not a close family member (a parent, grandparent, or sibling)—especially not her husband.

Yes. This means that for around twelve days every month (five minimum for menstruation, plus seven "clean" days—I won't get into how we reach those calculations here, it's too complicated) I cannot hug my husband or hold his hand or even pat him on the back.

And you thought it was horribly restrictive and frustrating that I can't hug *you!*

Remember when I told you I didn't want to get into the technical explanation about this before? Well, now I will explain. The touch restriction applies to anyone to whom one is sexually prohibited—except close family members. I'm sure that doesn't surprise you, but this will: the prohibition against premarital sex is actually *not* from the Torah; it is purely rabbinical. *But* any sexually mature woman who has yet to immerse in a mikveh, as with most unmarried religious Jewish women, is niddah, and therefore the restriction applies. And a woman who is *tehora*, but married, is obviously prohibited to anyone except her husband. So. Yeah.

Yes, I know it feels like a huuuuuuge stretch to think of any kind of physical contact as "coming close" to sexual relations, especially in a platonic friendship, and we've had that conversation before. As you know, some halakhic authorities permit leniency in cases of touch which is clearly for social formalities, such as shaking hands (and I tend to practice this in order to avoid embarrassing people). However, once you are friends, any kind of touch is inherently affectionate, and that's halakhically off limits.

And yes, I know it sucks. Have an e-hug.

Back to "family purity." The fact is that in a healthy, romantic relationship, there can be something really positive about this cycle of drawing apart and coming together again. Having limited time to be together can make you prioritize nurturing your physical relationship while it is permitted, and nurture the other aspects of your relationship while it is forbidden. Moreover, there is something in this period of "forbiddenness" that adds an aspect of yearning and desire. Niddah gives us an opportunity to long for each other. And that makes the eventual reunion that much sweeter and more meaningful and powerful.

Anyway. Where were we? Right, niddah. So once a woman completes her seven "clean" days, she must remove all physical barriers from her body and immerse in a mikveh. After she immerses, she is tehora, and she and her husband are permitted to be physically intimate again.

And *that*, as I'm sure you now understand, is why the mikveh is such a crucial part of any permanent Jewish community! The practice of family purity is one of the "Big Three" commandments that are central to observant Jewish life, and basically serve as a litmus test for whether one is halakhically observant or not. The other two are Shabbat and kashrut. Obviously, what goes on in other people's bedrooms is absolutely none of anyone else's business, so the latter two are generally how people identify each other as observant. I should also say that, along the observant spectrum, there are people who interpret "coming close to" more liberally, and don't have a problem with non-sexual physical contact. While I still must say that, unfortunately, I do not think that this interpretation falls within the halakhic framework, I still consider these people to be observant.

Conversion to Judaism

Immersion in the mikveh is the final step in the process of a halakhic conversion. Conversion to Judaism is a whole other topic for a whole other letter, so I won't elaborate on the rest of the process here, but immersion in the mikveh is the ritual act that changes that person's status. He or she goes into the water as a non-Jew, and emerges "reborn" as a Jew.

This probably reminds you of baptism, and in some ways it is an apt comparison. In both cases, there is some kind of immersion in water that creates an irreversible spiritual change in the religious identity of the individual. The major difference is that you can be "accidentally" or forcibly baptized, and the baptism is still binding. (As you know, this created some fairly problematic situations in the past.) Jewish halakhic (Orthodox) conversion, however, is impossible if you do not have a sincere intention to become a Jew and stay a Jew. If, at the moment of immersion, the potential convert does not intend to be Jewish and observe the Torah, the immersion is meaningless. If, however, one was totally sincere in that moment, but the next day changes one's mind and decides to be a Hindu, that convert is still a Jew—forever. Children can be converted, even as infants, but when they reach the age of halakhic responsibility (bar or bat mitzvah, age twelve for girls and thirteen for boys), they can protest the conversion. In other words, the conversion is conditional, depending on whether the child decides to continue being Jewish. So Jewish conversion can only happen with intention and consent, and under the supervision of a *beit din* (halakhic court).

Other Immersion

There are men (and non-Orthodox women) who immerse in the mikveh for spiritual or traditional reasons. While this is thought to be spiritually cleansing, particularly in Chassidic/Kabbalistic thought, it is not an immersion required by the Torah, so the whole "removal of barriers" is not required, and men may not recite the blessing for immersion. Men will immerse before visiting the Temple Mount, and many men will make a point of immersing before Yom Kippur (the Day of Atonement—see *Days of Awe*).

Love,
Daniella

Mikveh

Circumcision.
Wait! Don't Run Away Screaming!

Dear Josep,

    This Sunday we attended a circumcision ceremony for our friends' firstborn son, and it reminded me that this was one of the topics we originally agreed on discussing last year. You said we should save it for last among those topics, because it is "delicate," and I'll stick to my promise of no gory details! I have a fairly funny memory of when you first brought it up eight years ago, in the context of what is required for a conversion. I was like, "Do I seriously have to talk to this twenty-four-year-old male Christian about circumcision?! How did I get my nineteen-year-old religious Jewish female self into this?!" Well, eight years, a husband, and three sons later, I'm well over being shy about it!

    These days, circumcision has become one of those hotly debated early-parenting topics, alongside breastfeeding, birth choices, and vaccines. As I tentatively learned more about this debate, I understood that people circumcise their sons for a variety of reasons that have nothing to do with religion—health-related, social, or aesthetic. There was a period in history in which all boys were circumcised in the USA as a matter of public health policy. The health benefits, at least according to the current recommendations by the American Academy of Pediatrics, outweigh the risks of the procedure, but not by enough to recommend that it be done universally. Obviously, it is extremely daunting to imagine carrying out an irreversible surgical procedure on your son, even more so on his most sensitive parts, and many parents feel that it is cruel to do this without the child's consent. I totally hear that argument and it very well may be that, if I weren't Jewish and didn't believe God required it, I might not have chosen the procedure for my own sons. On the other hand, it is a fairly simple procedure when the child is a baby, which becomes more complicated and difficult when he's older, so it's more complex than just waiting to let him decide. The debate taps into all kinds of deeper issues, like what it means to be responsible for your children vs. respecting their autonomy, what it means to protect your children from harm, etc. Fascinating topic, but we're not going to get any further into it than that here.

Because, the fact is that I feel kind of outside of the debate. I circumcised my sons for one reason and one alone, which has no logical basis and therefore is basically non-debatable: "God said so." Genesis 17:10: "*This is My covenant, which you shall keep, between Me and you and your seed after you: every male among you shall be circumcised.*" (I mean, you can argue about the divine origin of the Torah, and whether God exists and all that, but that's a whole different conversation!)

Circumcision is one of those mitzvot that I feel test me and my commitment to Torah the most. It's really hard to stand there while someone intentionally hurts your tiny eight-day-old son, and listen to him cry in pain, and you can't do anything to comfort him. Of course, as the mother of a child who underwent three surgeries in his first four months of life and several more since, I have become a lot tougher about things like this. Sometimes you have to let someone hurt your child for his overall well-being. I believe circumcision is essential for his spiritual well-being, so I grit my teeth and get it done.

As I wrote about that awful Shabbat last year without power,[19] "Some mitzvot (commandments) are very hard to follow. Ultimately, our willingness to stay committed despite how difficult it is can bring us closer to Him, and Him closer to us. It is an eternal sign between us. Most times, it is a bed of petals. Occasionally, it is a bed of thorns. Ultimately, it is all roses."

Why would God ask us to do something like this? Well, circumcision is like kashrut in that it's a *chok*, the type of mitzvah without a logical explanation or given reason. So the answer is that we don't know. Some Sages teach that making a permanent physical mark on a part of the body that embodies our most base desires, is a symbolic expression and reminder to "master" those desires. The Maharal of Prague (Rabbi Judah Loew ben Bezalel) teaches an idea that I really connect to:

In Genesis 1:26, God says, "Let us make man in our image." There are many commentaries trying to explain why God used the plural in this statement. My favorite explanation is that God created us incomplete; the completion of our own creation is in our own hands. That is, He is inviting us to become a partner in our own creation. By making good choices and striving to be better and to seek Him, we complete ourselves. The Maharal explains that circumcision is a physical manifestation of this idea.

So what about women then, I hear you ask?

What, childbirth isn't enough?!

No, but, seriously, the Maharal says that women are created more whole spiritually and therefore do not need this physical completion.

On to the practicalities. What does a circumcision ceremony look like? (Wait!!! Don't run away! I *will* stick to my promise of no gory details! I'm not going to describe the procedure itself, I'm going to describe the ceremony around it. Okay? Are you breathing? Good.)

---

[19] See: *The Sabbath Keeps the Jews—Even When It Seems like It Doesn't.*

Circumcision

The circumcision is performed on the eighth day of the baby's life, barring any medical reasons to postpone it. In essence, the ceremony involves welcoming the baby to the Jewish people. So it begins with the congregation saying the words: "*Barukh haba*"—"Welcome." Though the obligation to circumcise one's son is on the baby's father, the procedure is usually carried out by a man called a *mohel*. There are mohels who are also doctors, but for the most part these are guys who have trained specifically to do circumcisions. I have heard that even gentiles sometimes prefer to have a mohel perform it because they are more experienced and well-trained in this particular procedure than most pediatricians. The mohel is also sort of the "master of ceremonies" and leads the congregation through the ceremony.

So the father brings the baby into the room—usually on a decorative pillow.

Some verses are recited responsively by the father and the congregation, and eventually the baby is placed on someone's lap, who is seated on the "Chair of Elijah." (This is usually a grandfather, uncle, or other loved one, whom the parents wish to honor with this role. There are lots of symbolic "honor roles" in the ceremony—who gets to pass the baby between the mother and the father, who gets to recite which blessing, etc.) The mohel performs the procedure—making a blessing beforehand, because it's a mitzvah—and then someone else reads a prayer blessing the baby and the parents, and announcing the baby's name. (You see, it is customary to wait until the brit to call the baby by his name, because he is not considered a part of the community until he has been circumcised. There is an idea that the parents have "divine inspiration" when they select the name for their children that borders on prophecy. We believe names have deep significance and affect the child's destiny. As you know, we put a lot of thought into our sons' names.) Usually, by this time, the baby is already calm. After the blessings have been recited, the baby is handed back to the mother. A festive meal follows... of course! No Jewish event is complete without food! In Ashkenazi communities, it's customary to serve bagels, because they are round, symbolizing the life cycle.[20]

The Sephardi/Mizrahi circumcisions I've attended involved a full-out feast with plenty of meat. In one I attended last year, celebrating the circumcision of the son of a couple of friends of North African descent, there were large platters of sweets and candies going around, and lots of songs I didn't recognize. But there was the same spirit of joy, lots of singing and clapping and dancing. It's really a joyful event, of welcoming a new baby into the community, and celebrating the new parents and/or big siblings.

So what about girls, I hear you ask? How are girls welcomed into the Jewish community?

Well, yes, there's much less pomp and circumstance around it. A female baby's name is usually announced during a Torah reading in the middle of a prayer service—on Monday, Thursday, or Shabbat. (I was born on a Monday before dawn, and my mother says my father went straight to prayer service and announced my name right then.) It is customary to hold a *simchat bat*, a "celebration for a girl," which is basically just a party. Some people make it more like a brit by reciting verses and waiting to announce the name on that day. I attended a really beautiful simchat bat like that once. But it's not really required by halakha, so people often put it off until the baby is a few months old, or indefinitely...

See? That wasn't so bad!

Love,
Daniella

---

[20] ...Don't think too hard about the symbolism.

Circumcision

On the Doorposts of Your Home: All About Mezuzot

Dear Josep,
So before I explain about *mezuzot*, I must first begin with the Shema prayer. Here is a translation of the full text of the first paragraph of the prayer:

> *Hear, O Israel, the Lord is our God, the Lord is One.*
> *You shall love the Lord your God with all your heart, with all your soul, and with all your might. And these words which I command you today shall be upon your heart. You shall teach them thoroughly to your children, and you shall speak of them when you sit in your house and when you walk on the road, when you lie down and when you rise. You shall bind them as a sign upon your arm, and they shall be as a reminder between your eyes. And you shall write them upon the doorposts of your house and upon your gates.*
> (Deuteronomy 6:4-9)

That last verse is the source for the mitzvah of mezuzah.
First of all: what is the Shema? Why is it so important? And why did God command us to say these words morning and evening, to bind them "as a sign upon your arm" and "a

reminder between your eyes,"[21] and to have them hanging at every doorpost?

The crux of the prayer is the opening verse. It is our declaration of allegiance to God, and our belief that He is one. The rest of the paragraph explains how that allegiance is manifested in our daily lives.

Okay, so we declare our allegiance to God. "The Lord is our God." Why, "the Lord is one"? What does his oneness have to do with our allegiance to Him and love for Him?

Well, first there's the obvious: we were the first nation to believe in the oneness of God, and this was our unique characteristic at the time. And though this may seem totally basic in a world so strongly influenced by the three monotheistic faiths, it's actually really not that intuitive an idea. When we look at the world, all we see is contrast. Everything is defined by its separation and distinction from everything else. A tree is not a rock. The sky is not the sea. Dark and light. Good and evil. These things are so mutually exclusive that it doesn't make sense at all that they could all truly be part of one unified thing. But they are. They are all God. This is a very difficult concept to grasp—so difficult that the ancient peoples assigned different gods to the different forces in the world. This made sense. Even the Christians felt a need to do this to some degree. Mainstream Christianity assigns all evil in the world to a being separate from God—the Devil—because God is supposed to be pure good; how could evil come from Him as well? But according to the concept of the Shema, this is a mistake. The good and the evil in the world are both a part of God, and all are part of the same reality, which is all ultimate good. This is very hard to understand.

But that concept is central to our mission in this world, and thus central to our identity as the Jewish people. Our mission in the world is to help reveal God's oneness and goodness, to lead the human race in its pursuit of Him, so that, together, we can bring the world to a point where He can bestow His

---

[21] Referring to tefillin. See: *Prayer, Part II*.

goodness entirely. **The message of the Shema is our raison d'être.**

And that is why we surround ourselves with its words. We recite it morning and evening. It is the first prayer we teach our children, and the last prayer we say before we die. (This is why you hear stories of Jews crying it out when facing death.) We bind it—physically or mentally—to our arms and minds when we pray. And, yes… we hang it on every doorpost.

If you look at the first verse of the Shema in a Torah or mezuzah scroll, you will see that the last letter of both the first and last words of the verse are enlarged. These two letters spell the word עד, "*ed*," which means "witness." Our mission in the world is to bear witness to God's oneness.

Okay, so that's the first paragraph of the Shema. What about the second paragraph? It reads like this:

It will be, if you will diligently obey My commandments which I command you this day, to love the Lord Your God and to serve Him with all your heart and with all your soul, that I will give rain for your land at the proper time, the early rain and the late rain, and you will gather in your grain, your wine, and your oil. I will give grass in your fields for your cattle, and you will eat and be sated. Take care lest your heart be lured away, and you turn astray and worship alien gods and bow down to them. For then the Lord's wrath will flare up against you, and He will close the heavens so that there will be no rain and the earth will not yield its produce, and you will swiftly perish from the good land which the Lord gives you. Therefore, place these words of Mine upon your heart and upon your soul, and bind them for a sign on your hand, and they shall be a reminder between your eyes. You shall teach them to your children, to speak of them when you sit in your house and when you walk on the road, when you lie down and when you rise. And you shall inscribe them on the doorposts of your house and on your gates—so that your days and the days of your children may be prolonged on the land which the Lord swore to your fathers to give to them for as long as the heavens are above the earth.

(Deuteronomy 11:13-21)

On the Doorposts of Your Home

Very similar to the first paragraph, but with one major difference: this one talks about the consequences of not loving God and not following the commandments. In Judaism, we talk about two motives for loving God: *ahava* and *yir'a*, love and awe (sometimes translated as fear, but awe is a better word for it). Both are important components of our service of Him, but love, obviously, is the highest level. The first paragraph of the Shema corresponds to ahava. It is unconditional. We love God with all our hearts and all our souls and therefore we perform these commandments. This is really ideal. But when we are not on that level, we need the second paragraph of the Shema, which corresponds to yir'a, so we perform the commandments out of fear of the consequences. The concept of Divine reward and punishment is very complex and I won't get into it now, but suffice to say that according to many Jewish philosophers such as Rabbi Chaim Luzzato, it is not as simplistic as it seems here.

There is a third and final paragraph of the Shema, but it is less relevant here because only the first two paragraphs are included in the mezuzah.

So what is the mezuzah? The word "mezuzah" actually means "doorpost." The mezuzah itself is a scroll of parchment on which the first two paragraphs of the Shema are inscribed on one side, and the word *Sha-dai* is inscribed on the other. Sha-dai is one of God's names in Hebrew, associated with kindness, and is also an acronym for *shomer dlatot yisrael*, "Guardian of the Doors of Israel." The scroll is rolled up from left to right with the words of the Shema on the inside. It is then affixed to the doorway. As you know, usually it is placed inside a nice protective case, one which has the letter ש or the word "Sha-dai" on it. Archeologists always know they have found a Jewish building when they see an indent carved into the doorway to hold the mezuzah.

The purpose of the mezuzah is, of course, to help us maintain an awareness of God and of our purpose in the world, every time we enter or exit a room.

The minimum halakhic requirement is to place one just on the main entrance of the home, but most of us affix a mezuzah in every doorway (except the bathroom, out of respect for the holy text) and also in buildings people don't live in, like office buildings. There is a custom to kiss it as we walk past; most of us do this by touching it and then kissing our hand. (You probably saw me do this a few times.) This helps us maintain an awareness of it, though it becomes something of an automatic reflex. Whenever I'm in a place with a doorway that doesn't have a mezuzah, I find myself automatically reaching for a mezuzah that isn't there! I call this "Phantom Mezuzah Syndrome."

The mezuzah is affixed to the upper third of the doorway, on the side that, upon entering the room, is to the right. The Ashkenazi custom is to affix it tilting toward the interior of the room; the Sephardi custom is to affix it vertically. Why the difference? Well, because, of course, there are differing opinions on the proper direction. According to one opinion, it should be vertical. According to the other, it should be horizontal. Sephardim go by the first opinion; Ashkenazim go by a compromise of both!

When affixing a mezuzah, the following blessing is recited: "*Blessed are You, Lord, our God, King of the Universe, who sanctified us with his commandments and commanded us to affix a mezuzah.*"

And with that, my friend, I bless you that only goodness, harmony and peace should cross your doorways, and awareness of God and His love for you should ever be in your mind.

Love,
Daniella

On the Doorposts of Your Home

Blessings:
Finding God in an Apple

Dear Josep,

You may have noticed that in many of my explanations about the way we perform certain commandments, I mention that we say a blessing beforehand, which always starts with the same formula: "*Blessed are You, Lord, our God, King of the Universe, who...*"

Reciting blessings is as regular a part of daily life as prayer. (Well, technically, it is, in itself, a form of prayer.) Most of the blessings I've mentioned are the kind we recite before performing a mitzvah. But there are other categories too, and in this letter I will address the different kinds of blessings.

But first, what do I mean by "blessing"? These "blessings" are short statements that express gratitude for something. So why are they called "blessings" and not, maybe, "thankings"? And even stranger, why do they all start with the statement, "Blessed are You"? Isn't it *we* who are blessed by *Him*? The Catholic grace before meals I have seen usually includes some form of, "Bless *us*, O Lord," not the other way around!

Well, first things first: what does the word "bless" mean, anyway? In Hebrew, the root that means "bless" is b.r.kh., and the Sages explain that it means "to increase" or "bring down Divine abundance." When I "bless" you, I am asking God to increase your health, wealth, happiness or whatever it may be, to shine His light on you... in essence, to give you more of Himself. So what could it possibly mean for me to "bless" God for creating the apple I'm about to eat?

The key to understanding this is to recognize the purpose of these blessings. It is not merely to show gratitude. The purpose of a blessing is **awareness**.

When I hold an apple in my hand and say, *"Blessed are You, Lord, our God, King of the Universe, who creates the fruit of the tree,"* what I'm really saying is a lot more than just "thanks for making this apple." I'm saying, "Your presence in this world has been made that much greater, has increased, through this fruit You created that I am about to enjoy."

I'm declaring that whatever it is I'm making the blessing for—whether it's a food I'm enjoying, a roll of thunder I heard, or a mitzvah I'm about to perform—is increasing God's presence in the world, through my recognition of His role in creating or commanding it.

So we're back to what I've always said is the main theme of Judaism: channeling the Divine into the mundane and revealing the spiritual through the physical. Through this worldly experience, I experience God; and when I declare that recognition, I make His presence in the world that much more known.

Very simply put: in this apple, I see God.

There are three main types of blessings.

Blessings of Enjoyment

These are blessings we make over something we enjoy with our senses. The most common ones are, of course, blessings over food. We recite blessings both before and after eating. There are different blessings for different categories of food: bread ("... *who brings forth bread out of the ground*"); grain products that are not defined as bread ("... *who creates different kinds of sustenance*"); wine ("... *who creates the fruit of the vine*"); fruit ("... *who creates the fruit of the tree*"), vegetables ("... *who creates the fruit of the ground*"); and everything else ("... *from whose word all came into being*"). If that sounds complicated, wait until I tell you that bananas and pineapples are halakhically "vegetables" because they are non-perennial plants... or that food can switch categories according to how it is prepared or eaten (for instance, orange juice). And don't even get me started on what defines a grain product as bread, or why we say "the fruit of the vine" for wine, but "the fruit of the tree" for grapes! The point is that to make the correct blessing, you have to have a basic awareness of how that food came to be on your plate. And making the blessing gives you an opportunity to reflect on this process. The apple came from a tree, which grew from the ground, thanks to sunlight and water and nutrients from the soil, and it's God who made all this happen.

"After" blessings are also divided by category: the long *birkat hamazon* ("blessing for sustenance"/"Grace After Meals") for after eating bread or a meal with bread (this is the blessing we made after the meal on Shabbat), a shortened version called *me'en shalosh* for grain products that are not bread, *or* fruits that fall under the category of the "Seven Species." These are the seven species referred to in Deuteronomy 8:8, the fruits that the land of Israel is especially celebrated for. They are: wheat, barley, grapes, dates, figs, pomegranates, and olives.

The last "after blessing" is *boreh nefashot*. It's one of the most disregarded blessings because it's so short, but in my view, it's one of the most beautiful and meaningful. It goes like this: "*Blessed are You... who creates numerous souls and their deficiencies; for all that You have created with which to maintain the life of every being. Blessed is He, the life of worlds.*"

The profundity of this blessing lies in its first section: "*who creates numerous souls and their deficiencies.*" Why would we be thanking God for creating a deficiency? Because the very reason we are thanking Him for giving us something to eat, is that He created hunger. If we were not hungry, we would not enjoy the fulfillment of that lack. Take this idea beyond physical sustenance, and you'll have a lot to think about.

Enjoyment blessings are also made on smelling something pleasant. These are very specific too, ranging from pleasant scents from flowers and trees, to the scent of herbs, to the scent of fruit, to the most specific—balsam oil. This, too, is a moment to pause and reflect on where this pleasant experience comes from, and use it to channel Godliness into the world.

Another blessing in this category is *shehechiyanu*: "*Blessed are You, Lord, our God, King of the Universe, who has granted us life, sustained us, and enabled us to reach this occasion.*" This is the blessing we make over new experiences (such as wearing new clothing) or occasions that are rare enough that we especially enjoy them when they come around (such as holidays, or eating the first fruit of a season).

Blessings for Commandments

Jews consider the Torah to be the greatest gift of all, and, as I've mentioned, the act of performing a mitzvah is an act of channeling Divine energy into the mundane. This is a very appropriate time to declare God's increased presence in the world through this act.

Blessings of Experience

They are called "blessings of sight" or "of hearing," but I'd call them "blessings of awe." These are the blessings we make when we see or hear something that reminds us of God's presence in the world. For example, when I hear a roll of thunder, I recite: "*Blessed are You, Lord, our God, King of the Universe, whose strength and might fills the world.*" When I see a streak of lightening, or experience an earthquake, or see an especially mighty mountain or river, I recite: "*... who performs an act of creation.*" When I see the Mediterranean Sea for the first time in thirty days, I say: "*... who created the Great Sea.*"

There is a special blessing for seeing a rainbow, which refers to the story of Noah: "... *who remembers the covenant, and is faithful in His covenant, and keeps His promise.*" The promise and covenant are: "*And it shall come to pass, when I bring clouds over the earth, and the rainbow is seen in the cloud, that I will remember My covenant, which is between Me and you and every living creature of all flesh; and the waters shall no more become a flood to destroy all flesh.*" (Genesis 9:14-15)

There is another special blessing that we make on flowering fruit trees, only during the month of Nisan (your birth month!): "*... who has made nothing lacking in His world, and created within it good creations and good trees for the sons of Adam to enjoy.*"

Another blessing of note is *Birkat HaGomel*; a blessing we say when we have been saved from a potentially life-threatening situation, such as surviving a dangerous illness or childbirth. We are required to say this blessing in front of at least ten people, because when God performs a miracle, we have an obligation to spread knowledge of it as much as we can. (This concept—*pirsumei nisa*, "publicizing the miracle" in Aramaic—is familiar from the holiday of Chanukah. We display our *chanukiyot* in a prominent window facing the street for this reason.) The person who was saved says: "*Blessed are You, Lord, Our God, King of the Universe, who bestows kindness upon the culpable, for He has bestowed kindness upon me.*" Those in attendance answer, "*Amen. May He who has bestowed kindness upon you, always bestow kindness upon you.*"

There are blessings for seeing an especially wise person; for seeing a king; for seeing a group of 60,000 Jews gathered in one place (which has to do with the number of Israelites gathered at Mt. Sinai); for seeing a place where a miracle happened for the Jewish people (such as the Red Sea, the walls of Jericho, or the Jordan river crossing); for seeing a place where a miracle happened to that individual or to his parents; for seeing especially beautiful people or creations, or for seeing especially unusual-looking people or creations... and for hearing good news, ("... *hatov v'hameytiv*," "...*who is good and does good*"), or bad news ("... *dayan haemet*," "... *the True Judge*.")

There is even a blessing for going to the bathroom! ("... *who created man with wisdom and created within him many openings and many cavities. It is exposed and known before Your Throne of Glory, that if one of them were to be ruptured or one of them were to be blocked it would be impossible to survive and to stand before You for even one hour. Blessed are You, Lord, Healer of all flesh who acts wondrously.*") As we are painfully reminded every time we have a stomach virus, properly functioning personal plumbing is definitely something to be grateful for!

Basically, as the rabbi in Fiddler on the Roof says, there truly is a blessing for everything.

Or should I say... *in* everything.

Because the whole purpose of making a blessing is to look deep into the world we live in, and find God in it.

Amen

When one hears someone else recite a blessing, one is required to answer "Amen." Ever wonder what the word "amen" means? The root of the word in Hebrew, א.מ.נ, a.m.n., is the same root as the word, אמונה, *emunah*, "faith." Basically, it's a statement that means, "What you say is true." When you answer "Amen," it is as if you had made the blessing yourself; you are confirming the declaration of the increase of God's presence, and thus, increasing awareness of God's presence yourself.

And now, of course, a blessing from me to you: may you always find God, even in the most mundane and unlikely places.

Love,
Daniella

Jewish Weddings

T̲HIS LETTER was originally sent to a number of friends, including Josep, shortly before my own wedding. What follows is an edited version.

Hi People!

Six days to the wedding!

I thought those of you unfamiliar with Orthodox Jewish weddings—whether you're attending or not—may like to know what it is we're up to these days. So, without further ado:

The Week Before

It is the custom, particularly in Ashkenazi communities, for the bride and groom not to see each other for the seven days leading up to the wedding. Eitan and I are also going to try not talking on the phone. I think the reason for this is obvious: to increase the longing for one another, and increase the euphoria when the bride and groom see each other again when he comes to cover her face with the veil (explanation to follow). A state secret: it also makes sure that the bride and groom don't have the opportunity to take out all their nerves on each other and have stupid little fights before the wedding.

In North African and Middle Eastern communities, there is a ritual celebration on the last day the bride and groom can see each other, called the *chinna*, after the spice henna. It involves traditional dress, foods, singing, and a ceremony involving a paste made from henna. (Since neither of us have an inkling of an ancestor from North Africa or the Middle East, we won't be doing that.)

In Ashkenazi custom, the Shabbat before the wedding is designated as a special Shabbat to celebrate the bride and groom. Many of my friends kick their families out of their houses and invite all their friends to celebrate Shabbat with them, and spend the day singing songs, playing games, and learning Torah in preparation for the wedding. I'm planning on having something very low-key and intimate instead, with just my local friends.

Eitan will have what's called an *aufruf*, in which he will be called up for an *aliyah*—a section of the Torah reading that takes place on Shabbat. In some communities, people throw candy at the groom when he finishes.

The Night Before

The bride goes to the mikveh—ritual bath—for the first time. In Sephardi communities, this turns into a big celebration, with lots of singing and candies and whatnot, but we Ashkenazim tend to be hush-hush about it (as everyone usually is about mikveh visits, because of the privacy surrounding the halakhic implications).

Starting the night before, the bride and groom each need a *milaveh* or *shomer* ("accompanier" or "guardian"), preferably a single friend, to be with him and her at all times. The *milavim* are in touch with each other throughout the day to make sure the bride and groom don't accidentally run into each other before the wedding ceremony. They also make sure the bride and groom have everything in order and taken care of so they don't need to worry about anything that day.

The Wedding Day

The day of the wedding is considered a *Yom Kippur Katan*, a "small Yom Kippur" for the bride and groom; a day on which all their past sins are forgiven, a day of rebirth and renewal. Therefore, the bride and groom each fast from the morning until either sundown or the *chuppah* (wedding canopy), whichever comes first. Eitan and I will be breaking our fast on the wine under the chuppah.

Also for that reason, it is customary for the bride and groom to recite the afternoon prayer of Yom Kippur instead of that of a normal weekday.

The Bride's Throne and the Groom's Table

As soon as the bride is dolled up and the reception starts, she greets the guests while sitting in the *kiseh kallah*, the "bride's throne." Guests approach and ask her for blessings and prayers for them and their loved ones. Prayers and blessings from a bride and groom on their wedding day are considered to carry special weight.

The groom sits around a table with the rabbi who is running the ceremony, family, and friends, and the *ketuba* (marriage contract) is drawn up and signed. This is called the *chatan's tish*.

Kisui Panim, or Bedecken ('Covering the Face')

When the chatan's tish is over, the guests begin a procession that leads the groom to the bride. The groom covers the bride's face with the veil, and then the father of the bride blesses her with a special blessing. The groom is then led to the chuppah by his father and future father-in-law (or sometimes his parents).

This time is considered a particular *et ratzon*, an auspicious time for prayer. The bride reads a special blessing while still sitting in the kiseh kallah as the groom reaches the chuppah and waits there. The chuppah is the wedding canopy—a cloth stretched between four poles, which symbolizes the new home the couple is about to build. Ashkenazim have a tradition to hold the chuppah under the open sky, as a symbol for the bride and groom to have children "as numerous as the stars in the sky" (as in God's blessing to Abraham in Genesis 15:5).

Chuppah V'Kidushin (The Wedding Ceremony)

When the bride is finished praying, her mother and future mother-in-law (or sometimes her parents) take her by the arms and the whole congregation accompanies her to the chuppah, sometimes in quiet, spiritual reverence, sometimes in joyful song and dance. (I'm gonna go for quiet and spiritual.)

The groom comes out from beneath the chuppah and accompanies the bride back underneath. In Ashkenazi custom, the bride circles around the groom seven times. Our rabbi explained to us that this is the bride's equivalent to the ring the groom puts on her finger—an act of "encircling" to single each other out. The custom is said to be based on a prophecy from Jeremiah 31:21: "*For God will create a new reality in the land, the female will encircle the man.*" The Sages understand this as meaning that women will actively look for their soulmates rather than waiting around for them (symbolizing the Jewish people actively searching for God), but the custom takes the literal meaning.

The Jewish wedding ceremony has two parts: *kidushin* or *irusin* ("sanctification" or "engagement") and *nisuin* ("marriage"). Many, many years ago, these two stages took place about a year apart, but because of a bunch of problems that created, they were put together, and now every wedding ceremony includes both, one after the other.

Kidushin

The rabbi makes a blessing over the wine, and the bride and groom drink. Wine is an integral part of any Jewish ceremony that involves holiness.

The groom makes a blessing, and then puts the ring on the right forefinger of the bride, with the statement, "*Harei at mikudeshet li k'dat Moshe v'Yisrael*"—"You are hereby sanctified to me by the law of Moses and Israel." In accepting the ring from the groom with that statement, the bride becomes "*mikudeshet*" or "sanctified," meaning that she is now forbidden to all men but her husband, though at this point she is forbidden to him also, because the second part of the ceremony hasn't been completed.

Sheva Brachot ('Seven Blessings')

The ketuba (marriage contract) is taken out and read aloud, mostly for the purpose of creating a *hefsek* (pause) between the two parts of the ceremony. The rabbi may also give a small speech at this time.

Then the *sheva brakhot* (seven blessings) are read, usually by a bunch of different guests the bride and groom wish to honor. The translation is as follows:

> Blessed are You, Lord, our God, King of the Universe, Creator of the fruit of the vine.

> Blessed are You, Lord, our God, King of the Universe, Who created everything for His glory.

> Blessed are You, Lord, our God, King of the Universe, Creator of man.

Blessed are You, Lord, our God, King of the Universe, Who created man in His image, in the pattern of His own likeness, and provided for the perpetuation of his kind. Blessed are You, Lord, the Creator of man.

Let the barren city be jubilantly happy and joyful at her joyous reunion with her children. Blessed are You, Lord, who makes Zion rejoice with her children.

Let the loving friends be very happy, just as You made Your creation happy in the garden of Eden long ago. Blessed are You, Lord, who makes the bridegroom and the bride happy.

Blessed are You, Lord, our God, King of the Universe, who created joy and celebration, bridegroom and bride, rejoicing, jubilation, pleasure and delight, love and brotherhood, peace and friendship. May there soon be heard, Lord our God, in the cities of Judea and in the streets of Jerusalem, the sound of joy and the sound of celebration, the voice of a bridegroom and the voice of a bride, the happy shouting of bridegrooms from their weddings and of young men from their feasts of song. Blessed are You, Lord, who makes the bridegroom and the bride rejoice together.

Raising Jerusalem Above Our Utmost Joy

The Jewish people is a joyful people, but our joy is never complete while our Temple no longer stands. As it says in the verse from Psalms: *"If I forget you, Jerusalem, let my right hand forget its cunning; let my tongue cleave to the roof of my mouth if I do not remember you, if I do not raise Jerusalem above my utmost joy."*

So, to close the wedding ceremony, we remember Jerusalem. The groom sometimes puts ashes on his head. He recites the above verse, many times in a song, and then he breaks a glass in memory of the Destruction of the Temple.

Funny fact: if you break a dish or a glass anywhere around Jews, they will probably start clapping and call out "Mazel tov!" ("Congratulations!") This is because the glass breaking is the last thing that happens under the chuppah, and usually when the groom breaks the glass, everybody bursts into cheers and song—not exactly the mood we were going for with the whole glass breaking thing, but there it is!

To avoid this, Eitan will break the glass in the middle of the solemn singing, so the breaking of the glass is connected to its proper context—the destruction of Jerusalem—and not to the happy one of finishing the wedding ceremony.

Together at Last

After the wedding ceremony, in Ashkenazi custom, the bride and groom are led to a room where they are allowed to be alone together in a locked room for the first time. This is called the *cheder yichud*.

According to Sephardi custom, once the bride and groom are in a locked room together, the bride must cover her hair, so many Sephardim don't do the cheder yichud and wait until after the wedding to be alone together. (Though I have a friend who just went ahead and covered her hair after the cheder yichud.)

After the bride and groom come out of the room, the dancing starts. It's a mitzvah to bring joy to a bride and groom, and the guests do their utmost—treating them like a king and queen, performing silly and/or complicated dances in front of them, etc.[22]

---

[22] I cannot tell you how many completely insane pictures of grown men and women doing, and wearing, ridiculous things I went through while

Sheva Brakhot/The Week After

Oh no. Don't think the festivities end when everyone goes home happy on the wedding night. We're talking about Jews, remember? One day of celebration for one of the most joyful occasions in a Jewish lifetime? Not a chance!

Each night, for six nights after the wedding (including the wedding, it amounts to seven days), a festive meal is held somewhere for the bride and groom. After the blessings following the meal, the Sheva Brakhot are read again (this is also true of the meal on the wedding night). That's why those parties are referred to as "Sheva Brakhot." In order to say the Sheva Brakhot, a minyan (quorum of ten men) is required, as well as at least one person who wasn't at the wedding or at any of the previous Sheva Brakhot.

And then life returns to relative normalcy, and the bride and groom live happily ever after as husband and wife.

I hope this has given you a clearer picture of what's coming up for me here, whether you're coming to the wedding or not.

Shabbat Shalom!
Daniella

---

searching for an illustrative photo for the blog. The guys at Eitan's yeshiva had this whole "amusing the bride and groom" thing down to an art; they brought puppets, wigs, silly hats, and other paraphernalia, and performed all kinds of crazy dances and acrobatics. My friends from college had prepared a wedding dance; my friends from my hometown invaded my closet and brought the accessories from my crazy Purim costumes from over the years, and a couple of them juggled eggs. Suffice to say, hilarity ensued.

Processing Grief:
Jewish Mourning Customs

Dear Josep,

Today is the 17th of Tammuz. Well, actually, it's the 18th, but that's what we call this fast, which was delayed by a day because of Shabbat. It marks the beginning of the Three Weeks, the period of mourning for the destruction of the Temple.

But before I talk about symbolic mourning, I should talk about actual mourning. So, um, yes, this is gonna be a downer. Pour yourself a glass of wine, 'cause I can't—I'm fasting!

As you know, my grandmother passed away at the end of March. My family is very blessed in that this was our first experience of needing to figure out the laws of mourning—*aveilut*—and how my mother was supposed to observe them. The *shiva* (explained below) was cut short because of Passover, and my mother's family is not the slightest bit religious, so the matter presented a number of issues.

But as a general rule, the customs around death and mourning in Judaism are designed to lead the mourners through a gradual process of grief and healing, and many report that this is helpful to them.

Burial

In Jewish law, we bury our dead as soon as possible. The reason for this is *kavod hamet*—"honoring the dead." According to Jewish beliefs, it causes the disembodied soul a lot of anguish and shame to see its former body lying there, exposed. In general, covering something is a sign of respect in our culture.

This is also the reason there is a lot of sensitivity around archaeology and the discovery of ancient Jewish cemeteries; we prefer to leave bones where they are and not expose them unnecessarily, and if there is a need to exhume them, this must be handled with utmost care and they must be reburied as soon as possible.

Jews are traditionally buried wrapped only in simple linen cloth. Coffins are not usually used, and if they are, the body is still completely wrapped in a shroud, again, out of respect for the dead. Men are usually buried with their tallit (prayer shawl—see *Prayer, Part II*).

There are a number of prayers that are standard for funerals. It's customary to read psalms, and the rabbi or leader of the funeral recites *E-l Maleh Rahamim*: "God, Full of Mercy," the prayer for the dead.

The close family members also perform *kriya*, a symbolic rending of one's clothes to express their grief.

Kaddish

I have briefly mentioned Kaddish before, and here is the place to elaborate. Kaddish is a prayer in Aramaic. It appears during the prayer services in a number of forms, most of them recited by the chazzan, the prayer leader. It can only be recited in the presence of a minyan, a quorum of ten men. Sometimes, however, it is recited by anyone in the congregation who has lost a parent over the past year. This is known as the Mourner's Kaddish.

So what is this prayer and why is it something that mourners traditionally recite? Here's a translation of the Ashkenazi version of the Mourner's Kaddish:

Glorified and sanctified be God's great name.

Throughout the world which He has created according to His will; may He establish His kingdom in your lifetime and during your days, and within the life of the entire House of Israel, quickly and soon; and say, amen.

May His great name be blessed forever and to all eternity. Blessed and praised, glorified and exalted, extolled and honored, adored and lauded be the name of the Holy One, blessed be He.

Beyond all the blessings and hymns, praises, and consolations that are spoken in the world; and say, amen.

May there be abundant peace from Heaven, and life, for us and for all Israel; and say, amen.

He who creates peace in His celestial heights, may He create peace for us and for all Israel; and say, amen.

A beautiful prayer, for sure. But what does all this praising God have to do with mourning?

I heard three interesting answers to this question. The first one is that when someone dies, they are unable to continue to perpetuate the good and Godliness that they were able to in their lifetime, and when their loved ones say Kaddish, a very holy prayer about the might and glory of God, they "fill in" some of the vacuum of goodness that that person left behind.

We have a concept called *ilui neshama*, the "raising of a soul." We believe that we, the people who were affected by the departed, can continue to perpetuate his or her good in the world, by doing good deeds in his or her merit. We believe that this assists the soul in its process of "spiritual cleansing" that occurs in the afterlife.[23] Reciting Kaddish is one very important way to "raise a loved one's soul." People also teach or study Torah classes, put together charities, or sponsor structures, objects, or projects for the community in memory of someone for this purpose.

I think there is a very profound idea there about the effect we have on other people and how that effect, in turn, affects us and our spiritual "health." The living loved ones can carry on the legacy and positive influence of a soul that has departed.

Another explanation for why the Kaddish is recited under these circumstances, is one that my mother heard from her meditation teacher and rabbi (she calls him her "Meditation Rebbe"), Rabbi James Jacobson-Meisels. He talks about the line, "*Beyond all blessings and hymns...*" The word for "beyond" (or more accurately, "above") in Aramaic is *"l'ayla,"* and during the holiest time of the year, the Ten Days of Repentance, we repeat this word during Kaddish: *"l'ayla u'l'ayla,"*—"above and beyond." Rabbi James teaches that the Kaddish is about God's vastness and greatness and holiness and kindness, above and beyond anything we can imagine or describe; *beyond all blessings and hymns that are spoken...* we have no words for the greatness of God and His love. In the context of this greatness, Rabbi James teaches, what is my grief, and what is my sadness? A small blip in the general experience of God's universe. Maybe, he says, the Kaddish is recited to help give us that perspective.

The third answer, and the one that speaks to me the most, is that when we say Kaddish, we are speaking for the departed. You see, when we die, and rise above our human understanding of the universe, we see God in all His glory, and if there is one thing we want to tell the people we left behind on Earth, it is how truly exalted and glorious God is, "*beyond all blessings and hymns*"... but the dead can't tell us this. So we, their loved ones, become their voice, telling the world of God's greatness,

---

[23] See *The Vagueries of the Jewish Afterlife*.

and blessing us all with peace and redemption—"*in your lifetime and during your days.*"

Sitting Shiva

"Shiva" means "seven." This refers to the custom of spending seven days in intense mourning following the burial of a close family member. It is called "sitting shiva," because part of the custom is to sit on low benches, stools, or the floor (as opposed to chairs or couches) and to stay in the "shiva house" for the duration of the shiva. (Ideally, the shiva should take place in the house of the deceased, and all members of the immediate family should try to stay there for the week; but if this is problematic, the home of one of the mourners is fine, and the other mourners can come sit there most of the day and then go home to sleep.)

Ideally, the mourners should not have to leave the house at any time during the shiva. I'm sure you're familiar with how painful and difficult it is to "put on your public face" and go out of the house when you're dealing with something very difficult. We don't want the mourners to have to do this. The community must come together and run their errands for them. Their friends, neighbors, and other family members do the shopping, cooking, and cleaning for them. (When there's a shiva house in our community, someone sets up a Google Doc excel sheet to schedule meals to bring to the mourner's home during the week. Almost every time I've tried to sign up, it was completely full by the time I got to it.) This custom compels the community to embrace and support the mourner.

Other customs for mourners include: covering the mirrors (to symbolize turning inwards and away from physicality), not shaving or cutting hair, refraining from eating meat or drinking wine, refraining from marital relations, not wearing leather shoes, and not washing for pleasure.

Processing Grief

Making a Shiva Call

It's not only customary, but a mitzvah, for members of the community to come to the shiva house and pay a visit to comfort the mourners. *Nichum aveilim*, comforting mourners, is a very important mitzvah in Judaism. It can be a very difficult one, too. A few years ago, the husband of a friend from our community died very suddenly and tragically. He was a young guy in his early thirties, with a successful bakery business and three young kids. The enormity of the tragedy was just unfathomable. As a young mother myself, with three young kids, and a husband more or less his age, I was deeply affected by this death, and I knew that if I went to the shiva I'd just fall apart. But I knew that I should go anyway. I sat on one of the benches opposite my friend, and just cried and cried. When the time came to go, I went over to her, and I was so overcome with sadness I could hardly force out, in a voice so strained it came out a most inelegant squeak, "I have no words. Only tears," before dissolving into sobs again. I felt awful because I was the only one crying at the time, and I feared that my deep sadness just reopened the wounds for everyone there. But the shiva is exactly the time and the place to fall apart, and I hope that my expression of grief at least gave some legitimacy to the inexpressible feelings of others who were there. In any case, my friend, who seemed completely drained of tears at that point, asked me if I remembered when he had brought us food they'd cooked for us when my youngest son was born. I told her that I remembered, and kissed her hands, and rose to leave and compose myself.

When visiting a shiva house, there are some important rules about protocol. The most important one is that you must not speak to the mourner unless he or she specifically expresses a desire to speak to you. Someone who is grieving should have the liberty to choose if and when he or she wants to speak, and about what. Often, the conversation at a shiva involves speaking about the person who passed away, telling stories about him or her, passing around pictures, and sharing memories. This helps the mourners process the loss. But if they prefer to sit in total silence, they should be able to do that, and still experience the love and support of the community. There are no words to comfort someone who has just experienced a loss.

When leaving a shiva house, it's customary to approach the mourner, and recite the following traditional statement: "*May the Omnipresent comfort you among the mourners of Zion and Jerusalem.*" This expresses our sense of family, and our collective mourning and loss.

When the shiva is over, the comforters who are with the mourners at the time accompany them on their first symbolic walk out of the house. This is the gradual transition back to normal life, and we don't want the mourners to have to do this alone.

The Shloshim

After the shiva, there is a period of lighter mourning. It is called the "*shloshim,*" the "thirty," because it usually lasts thirty days (including the seven days of shiva). They still do not shave or cut their hair during this time, and avoid social events, especially ones during which music is played. The purpose of this is also to ease the mourner out of mourning and back into normal life. It is expected that, during this period, someone who has experienced a loss will still have periods of intense grief, and the circle of family and friends should be supportive of this.

When mourning a parent, the period of lighter mourning lasts a year. There are a number of explanations for this, and I think it makes sense that the mourning for the person who gave you life should be more intense and last longer than mourning for another family member. Kaddish is recited for all but the last month of that year.

Annual Remembrances

Every year on the date of the loved one's death, there is a custom to visit the grave site, light a candle,[24] and recite prayers. In Yiddish, this is called the *yehrzeit*.

There is also a special prayer, called *Yizkor* ("He will remember") to commemorate the dead during prayer services on Yom Kippur, Shmini Atzeret, the last day of Passover, and Shavuot. Usually, members of the congregation who don't have someone to pray for during this prayer leave the synagogue while it is recited. This was the first year that my mom said the prayer, and it was very soon after the loss, so it was pretty tough. But she told me she had a friend there to hold her hand and hug her and get her through it.

May we know only joy and good news.

Love,
Daniella

---

[24] More on memorial candles in *A Nation of Pyromaniacs*.

Jewish by Choice: The Ins and Outs of Halakhic Conversion

Dear Josep,

    I recently had a discussion with a friend of mine who was adopted as a baby and was raised in a Reform Jewish family in the USA. When she participated in Jewish events at college, she was dismayed to find that the Orthodox Jewish rabbis there welcomed her as a "good friend to the Jews," but not as an actual Jew. I expressed that I was sorry to hear that she felt they were looking down on her, and described how the Orthodox interpretation of Jewish law makes things tricky; that it's hard to hold the paradox of believing 100% in the authority of Jewish law, but also believing 100% in one's right to define oneself, and 100% honoring one's upbringing as a Jew.

    She expressed interest in hearing more about the halakha on the matter, and I thought, "I feel a letter to Josep coming on."

    So, let's take it from the top:

Who Is a Jew by Birth?

    This is the subject of much controversy, especially relevant in a country where your eligibility for citizenship depends on whether you are officially defined as a Jew. The Law of Return, which defines who is considered Jewish for Israeli citizenship purposes, is not a halakhic definition. You can become an Israeli citizen if you have a Jewish parent or grandparent, or if you are married to someone who falls under that definition. You cannot become an Israeli citizen if you were born to a Jewish parent or grandparent, but voluntarily changed your religion.

The halakhic definition of a Jew by birth is someone who was born to a Jewish mother. According to halakha, it does not matter if you convert to another religion—once you are Jewish, you are a Jew forever. But in order to be considered a Jew, you must either be born to a Jewish mother, or convert.

While I know it's not very politically correct, I see it as great wisdom (divine or rabbinic, whichever you think the law came from) to invest the responsibility of carrying on Jewish heritage specifically in the hands of mothers. You see very clearly in crypto-Jewish families that it was the women who passed on the traditions and raised their children as secret Jews. Think about it: almost all of those strange remnants of Jewish traditions you find in crypto-Jewish families are practices upheld primarily by women. Practices to do with cooking, like checking eggs for blood, burning a small amount of dough when baking bread, separating milk and meat, etc.; sweeping toward the center of the room; lighting Shabbat candles in secret—these are historically all part of a woman's domain. It is not the only time the Torah acknowledges women as having more of a natural tendency to be faithful to God and the Torah.

This Awesome Stuff Is Mine

There is a cartoon on The Oatmeal called "How to Suck at Your Religion."[25] While I'm not a particular fan of the condescending attitude or the crude humor, it has some good points, and there is one part that is relevant to our discussion:

---

[25] This can be found at: http://theoatmeal.com/comics/religion

"This is why I'm a fan of Buddhists and Jews. Their attitude is more like 'I'm Jewish and this s*** is awesome. I don't give a raging crap if you're joining or not. In fact, you're not *allowed* in. This awesome s*** is *mine*.'"

Well, some might feel the opposite about the exact same thing, and claim that we are elitist snobs who think we are in some kind of special club that nobody can join. But that's not true. You can join. We just don't see any reason you should.

We believe that all nations and religions have their own place in the world and their own special mission, and we have no problem with them as long as they observe the seven Noahide Laws, which are the most basic laws of moral conduct (banning murder, sexual immorality, cruelty to animals, theft, idolatry, and cursing God, and requiring the establishment of a justice system to uphold the previous six). We don't believe that keeping the Torah and all the obligations required of us as Jews is relevant to most of humanity, and we don't think it makes sense to take on all these extra obligations when they are not required of you. Moreover, we'd rather not make someone into a Jew only to have him not keep the Torah. So, unlike the other major religions, we do not actively encourage conversion; we actually discourage it.

Basically, according to Orthodox law, you can only convert to Judaism if you absolutely cannot see yourself living any other way. And we have a specific policy to discourage converts—we call it "dissuasion"—which often manifests in making things more difficult than they have to be. You have to really, really want it.

What Does a Halakhic Conversion Entail?

First of all, living as a halakhically observant Jew, as I certainly hope you have gathered by now, requires a *lot* of knowledge. You have to know how to properly observe Shabbat, getting into the minute details of the actions that are and are not forbidden. You have to know how to properly observe kashrut (about which I had to write *three* letters to list the very basics). You have to know how to pray, what blessings to say on what, how to observe each of our bajillion holidays... the list goes on and on. My husband was not raised Orthodox, and he can attest to the difficult learning curve he went through after deciding to become religious. So the first thing you need to do when contemplating conversion, is **study**.

A **lot**.

The duration of studying for conversion depends on the individual. For some, it can take a few months; for some, more than a year or even two. But it's not enough to study in classes; you have to be immersed in a Jewish community and learn through practice, by seeing and experiencing life as a halakhically observant Jew. So potential converts usually have "adoptive families" in the community that take them in, host them for Shabbat and holidays, and generally teach them organically the way a child learns to observe the mitzvot from his family.

When the potential convert reaches a level of knowledge that would allow her to observe halakha fully, she appears before a panel of rabbinic judges, a beit din, who drill her on her knowledge of Judaism and halakha. If they rule that she is knowledgeable and sincere, she then goes to immerse in the mikveh, after which she is considered a full Jew.

I used "she" in the previous paragraph even though it applies to men as well, because for men, there's an extra step. Before immersing in the mikveh, male converts also must undergo circumcision. Obviously, this is not as simple a procedure as it is for an eight-day-old baby; it's done in a medical setting with local anesthesia. Well, you ask, what about men who were already circumcised? After all, many non-Jewish parents choose to circumcise their sons for medical or aesthetic reasons. The problem is that the circumcision must be performed by a Jew, with the intent of fulfilling the mitzvah. So, if the original intent of the circumcision was medical or aesthetic, the male convert undergoes a ritual procedure of drawing a drop of blood from the area. This spiritually "repurposes" the procedure as a mitzvah.

What About Children?

The rule about the maternal line determining whether a child is a Jew applies at the moment of birth. So if a woman converts while pregnant, the child she gives birth to as a Jew is considered Jewish. However, if she converts after she has already had children, even tiny babies, they must undergo conversion, too. But because a child is not obligated in the mitzvot yet, there is no requirement to appear before a beit din. Moreover, **a Jewish conversion has to be completely voluntary**, but a child is not considered by halakha to have moral agency until he or she comes of age (bar/bat mitzvah—thirteen for a boy, twelve for a girl). So the conversion of a child is basically this: he or she is ritually immersed in the mikveh, and raised as a Jew. But when bar or bat mitzvah, he or she can choose whether s/he wants to "accept the yoke of Torah" or not. If the child decides s/he is Jewish, the symbolic conversion as a child stays in effect and the child is considered completely Jewish. If s/he doesn't want to be Jewish, the conversion is retroactively annulled.

In terms of adoption, a child who was not born to a Jewish biological mother is not considered Jewish by halakha, even if s/he is adopted and raised by a committed Jewish family. So in this case s/he needs to undergo conversion, as above.

Gray Areas

I heard of a case recently where an entire family of ultra-Orthodox Jews found out that they were not actually halakhically Jewish because their maternal ancestor had not undergone what their rabbinic authority considered a proper conversion. Since it was clear that they intended to keep halakha and had adequate knowledge of it, they did not have to appear before a beit din; they just immersed in the mikveh.

In cases where there is some doubt about whether a conversion was performed properly, the person may choose to undergo a *giur l'chumra*, a "conversion for the sake of stringency." It would basically be a condensed version of the conversion process, without the "dissuasion."

What About Conservative and Reform Conversions?

The Conservative movement has a similar process of conversion, and, in the past, since the people who sat on the Conservative *batei din* (rabbinic panels) often kept Shabbat and kosher to Orthodox standards, some Orthodox authorities considered those conversions to be valid. Nowadays, it's trickier, and usually, if someone underwent a Conservative conversion and wants to become Orthodox, he or she may choose to undergo another conversion under Orthodox supervision.

Reform conversions are different, varying from community to community on the exact procedure. They are generally not recognized by the Conservative movement, and are definitely not recognized by the Orthodox.

All Is Not Rosy

I have to add, from first-hand accounts, that the rabbinic courts can make life very, very difficult for converts or for adoptive parents, and unnecessarily so. There are sometimes a lot of ugly politics, and this problem is tenfold in Israel, where the Rabbinate holds the authority over marriage, divorce, and conversion, and can be picky about whose conversions they accept as valid. (Marriages between people of other religions are handled by their religious authorities.) If the Rabbinate does not consider you Jewish, you can't marry a Jew in Israel. Couples like this often travel to Cyprus or elsewhere to get married.

The issue of who is considered halakhically Jewish, especially in a world where a majority of Jews do not follow halakha and accept a more liberal definition of Judaism, is a very sensitive and sticky issue for all involved. The point of conflict for the friend I mentioned at the top of the post is that she was born to a non-Jewish biological mother, and adopted by a Reform family that did not believe there was any need to convert her. So her family, her community, and, of course, she herself, define her as Jewish, but halakha does not. I can only imagine how infuriating and demeaning it must feel to have somebody tell you that according to their beliefs, you are not what you have always known you are. I wish there were a more comfortable middle ground.

Love,
Daniella

Jewish by Choice

Women in Orthodox Judaism, or: Daniella Opens a Can

Dear Josep,

I was asked recently whether I had written anything for the blog on the status of women in Judaism. I gave an ironic smile and said, "Oh, heck, no. I've been avoiding *that* can of worms."

Well... I brought my can opener.

I've been avoiding it because... well, volumes have been written on the topic of women and gender in Judaism from every possible viewpoint and perspective, and I don't feel I have anything groundbreaking to contribute to the conversation. Furthermore, my views on the topic are somewhat conflicting and in flux—sometimes I feel one way strongly, and sometimes another, and sometimes neither.

But you're not part of any of that discourse, so I might as well just give it to you straight, and then discuss my thoughts on it afterwards.

The Torah asserts a fairly politically-incorrect, but in my opinion, actually-correct idea: that men and women are built differently. Now that isn't to say that one gender is better than the other, or that some men aren't built more similar to women, and some women more similar to men. It means that, in general, the biological difference reflects a mental and spiritual difference, too. And the differences in the requirements of halakha in regards to men and women, are meant to reflect those differences.

However, as we all know, society has been abusing those differences since the dawn of humanity, and some of the differences between men's and women's roles in society are the result of misogyny and abuse of power. Sadly, there are some aspects of Jewish law that probably reflect that as well.

Practically speaking, the difference is this: women have fewer halakhic requirements, and therefore fewer halakhic privileges, than men. We are exempt from the commandments that are anchored to a certain time of day, and a few others. They include many of the external and public ritual observances, such as prayer, putting on tefillin, studying Torah, and the like. While that means we have less halakhic "responsibility," it also means that we can't be as involved in those rituals as men are. For example, because we're not required to study Torah, and therefore hearing the Torah reading is optional for us, we can't read the Torah for a man to fill his obligation, because he needs to hear it from someone who has the same level of obligation as him. When it comes to the reading of the Scroll of Esther on Purim, on the other hand, women and men are equally obligated, and therefore a woman could theoretically read it for a man and fill his obligation. But because of issues of modesty, it is very rare for a woman to read megilla for men (even though it is permissible). In communities that have megilla readings by women, they are usually for women only.

So, historically, the combination of lesser obligation and modesty issues led to women being marginalized in the synagogue, and left out of the houses of learning altogether until quite recently. Women were generally your typical homemakers and childbearers, and female leaders were very rare. But they did exist! Miriam, Moses' sister, had a prominent role among the Israelites. Deborah the Prophetess (Judges 4-5) led a war against a Canaanite general. Salomé Alexandra (*Shlomtzion* in Hebrew) was a Hasmonean queen who brought relative peace to Judea under her rule. A woman called Bruriah is quoted as a Sage in the Talmud, and was respected for her vast knowledge. And today, there are quite a number of rebbetzins (rabbis' wives) who are regarded as great spiritual leaders.

Still, as a general rule, women have a more traditional role in Jewish society, and the laws of modesty tend to focus more on women's requirements than men's. There is no denying that sometimes that can be stifling, if not discriminatory.

However. There are a few "howevers":

Unlike most other religions, the heart of Judaism is not actually the external rituals observed in the synagogue, but the laws observed in the home, namely kashrut, Shabbat, and family purity. The observance of these laws has always fallen mostly in the domain of women. Moreover, having children and raising them as dedicated Jews has a lot of importance to us. Therefore, women have actually had a very central role in Judaism. That's one of the reasons Judaism is passed down through the mother, not the father or a combination of both.

Which brings me to the next "however": there are aspects of Jewish law that actually favor women over men, such as what I just mentioned. Another example: the Jewish marriage contract is slanted sharply in favor of the woman. The Torah (Exodus 22:10) explicitly requires a husband to provide for his wife, and it specifies: food, clothing, and sexual satisfaction! While the husband does expect certain "rights" from his wife, these have much less weight than those three Torah obligations. The entire contract was built to protect women, and though it's far from perfect, it was way ahead of its time.

Also... things are changing, even in the most insular of Jewish communities. It was always accepted for women to have female spiritual leaders, but now that has become a lot more widespread, and there's even a daring movement in the Orthodox world to ordain female rabbis. Whereas many synagogues used to designate one little room in the back with a little window as the "women's section," these days it's much more common to have a barrier down the middle of the room, so the women can be close to the ark where the Torah scrolls are kept, and follow the prayers more easily. In the communities I've belonged to, women also give talks on Torah topics during the services (where only men used to do that) and generally participate more fully in the ritual aspect of Jewish life. I read from my weekly Torah portion at my bat mitzvah party (instead of at synagogue) and a number of my peers held women's prayer services for their bat mitzvahs so they could read from the Torah during the service. I've been reading from the Scroll of Esther on Purim during women's readings since I was in tenth grade.

Personally? I've very rarely felt excluded and marginalized as an observant Jewish woman. I grew up in communities where women were respected and valued. But I recognize that I may not be representative of the majority. I mean... I grew up with a mom who is a karate instructor and who later became a prominent activist for women's empowerment and all kinds of other cool things; she is one of the founders of El Halev (the Association for Women in the Martial Arts in Israel). And I followed in her footsteps as a self-defense instructor.

Basically, I was raised in a household where there was no concept that I was any "less" because I was a woman. My mother always took a very active role in her public practice of Judaism. I went to a high school for religious girls, and they never gave me a sense that I had any less responsibility or a less important place in society than men. For the most part, I am relieved to have a "lesser" obligation toward certain mitzvot, because it gives me more leeway, and freedom to connect to God in a way that suits me. And I connect to the more "feminine" aspects of Judaism and the commandments that have traditionally been embraced as being "women's" commandments—lighting Shabbat candles, taking challah (separating a piece of dough and burning it in memory of a donation to the priests that would have been made in the time of the Temple), and immersing in the mikveh. In general, I grew up with the sense that women are to be respected and revered for our power to bring life into the world; that femininity is a force

Letters to Josep

that is different, but no less powerful, than masculinity, and both are required to bring balance to the world.

I know, though, that there are many who have experienced being a Jewish woman differently.

I've mentioned to you before that there are things about the Torah that I struggle to reconcile with my own sense of morality. In some senses, we believe that the wisdom of the Torah is Divine and therefore eternal and relevant at every moment in time. In other senses, however, we recognize that some parts of it may have been meant as a compromise with human nature, taking into account the context of the time. For example, in Deuteronomy 22:1-14, the Torah describes a situation of war, in which a beautiful woman is taken hostage by an Israelite soldier. The Torah permits the Israelite to sleep with her, but only after he fulfills the following conditions:

1) He must admit her into his household.
2) Her head must be shaved and her nails cut.
3) She must be permitted to wear regular (non-slave) clothing.
4) She must be given a full month to mourn the loss of her parents.

After all these things, if he still wishes to sleep with her, he may marry her, and do so. If not, he must set her free, and he is not allowed to sell her, because the Torah says, "he has tormented her."

... Why would the Torah allow a Jew to "torment" a woman this way?

The Sages teach that during the time of the Bible, and even today (see: Daesh) raping and pillaging as part of war was a matter of course. The Torah accepts that this is the reality, the Sages say, and that this is part of human nature during wartime; however, it seeks to channel this urge more positively. Meaning, it gives the man an outlet for his urge, but only under certain circumstances that place some distance between him and his urge, reducing the harm to the woman somewhat, and discouraging him from doing this in the first place.

But why, one would ask, would the Torah do this? If the Torah recognizes wartime rape as immoral, why not simply forbid it? The Sages would respond that the Torah has to take human nature into account, because if it ordered us to do things that were simply impossible, we would end up rejecting the whole thing.

Okay, well, I recognize the wisdom in taking human nature into account. But why is wartime rape "channeled," while, say, homosexual relations are completely forbidden? And I think the answer is that the Torah was speaking to the context of its time—when homosexuality was less about love and more about idol worship, and women were still viewed as lesser members of society, if not property.

The fact is that the Torah was daringly progressive for its time in terms of its treatment of women. As far as I know, it was the first religion to grant women any rights at all. (See above about Jewish marriage.) Many of the laws, such as requiring a man to marry a woman if he rapes her, seem cruel and primitive in the context of our time, but actually made more sense in the context of the Biblical period; a woman who was raped was seen as damaged goods and would probably never find a husband to provide for her—pretty much a death sentence for a woman of that period. Requiring the rapist to marry her meant that she would be provided for. "Well, then," I say, "why not punish rape more severely, and require the community to support a woman who was raped, or offer an incentive to a man who marries a victim of rape?" I have lots of "advice" for God, you see...

I'm not the only person, however, to think that the restrictions in the Torah are sometimes not enough, and that the rules should be adapted to raise the moral standard. The most famous example of this is the ban of Rabbenu Gershom, prohibiting Jews from marrying more than one wife. While polygamy was not prohibited by the Torah, monogamy was generally the norm in Jewish society, and Rabbenu Gershom, seeing how much harm polygamy could cause, made it officially prohibited in the 11th century.

The problem is that this only goes in one direction. We can add restrictions, but we can't lift them. So if monogamy makes sense, we can definitely forbid men to marry more than one wife. And if slavery is awful, we can toss the laws protecting the rights of slaves and ban slavery altogether. But if, say, it also makes total sense for women to serve as rabbinical judges, we can't cancel the strong precedent in Jewish law that asserts that rabbinical judges must be male (based on the conjugation of the Biblical passage). It is those types of restrictions or limits that are the source of the most friction in this constant conflict within the heart of the modern observant Jew. Jewish law does change and shift over time and there is importance to the reality on the ground, but there is a strong anchor in ancient texts that may be less relevant to our time... and that's built in to the system.

So I think that the Torah was meant as a starting point; a blueprint on which the Oral Tradition and the living sea of Jewish law was meant to be built upon. And I think that there are parts of it that are meant to be taken at face value—such as, "Thou shalt not murder"—and others that we are *meant* to struggle with over time. So maybe God actually likes my "advice," and gives me—and all people in general—the responsibility to figure these things out, working from the framework laid out by the Torah. And maybe the things we find difficult, we're supposed to find difficult. I don't know why. But I have faith that God knew what He was doing.

Our anchor in ancient texts and precedents, which in some ways may hold us back, also prevents us from being swept away in the swiftly-changing currents of human ideas. This may be counterintuitive to the modern thinker, but there's great wisdom in it, because the human sense of morality has shifted drastically over time—usually in a direction of greater morality, but not always. Western concepts of equality and human rights, for example, are wonderful and progressive ideas that are definitely supported by the Torah. Western concepts of sexual freedom, however, can be highly destructive when they get out of bounds—objectifying women, creating an environment where young men feel they have to make sexual conquests to be "real men," etc. When you have a system like ours, trends and ideas are sifted through many filters and considered extremely carefully, before we adopt them as part of our society. So, being slow to change has its advantages, too.

And now that I've probably offended or disappointed everyone along the entire religious and political spectrum, I'm just gonna go put this can opener away...

Love,
Daniella

The Jewish Year

The Jewish Year

As mentioned in the letter on Shabbat, in Judaism we have a concept that certain points in time have inherent sanctity. Shabbat is the most common example, occurring once a week. However, the Jewish calendar is full of holidays, each one focusing on a different aspect of our relationship with God and with the rest of the Jewish people.

In Judaism, we think of time as a cycle. A week begins on Sunday and ends on Shabbat, and then a new week begins. A month ends on the 29th or the 30th day, and then a new month begins with a day we call Rosh Chodesh, celebrated with festive prayers. The year begins with Rosh Hashana, but the cycle of the months actually begins in Nisan, taking us from our birth as a nation (celebrated on Passover) through our reception of the Torah (Shavuot), to our acceptance of God's kingship (Rosh Hashana) and judgement (Yom Kippur), and finally basking in God's presence (Succot and Shmini Atzeret). There are lesser Jewish holidays in the months that follow: Chanukah, celebrating a spiritual and military victory over the Greeks, and Purim, celebrating our rescue from an evil Persian decree... and then the cycle begins again. The hope is that these cycles will not be circles, coming around to the same point at which we began; but rather spirals, circling up to a

The Jewish Year

higher level and meeting each holiday with new spiritual maturity and insight.

The Jewish calendar is lunar, but influenced by the solar. The Jewish Sages add days to certain months during some years, and an entire month during a leap year, in order to be sure that Passover falls in the spring (as required by the Torah). If the calendar were only lunar, like the Muslim calendar, our holidays would cycle around the year, like theirs do.

In this section, we will start with a letter that gives a general overview of the Hebrew calendar, and then explore each of the Jewish holidays, starting with the High Holidays.

Your Personal Jewish Calendar

Dear Josep,

You once asked me where you could find a Hebrew calendar to help you keep track of the holidays and stuff, since, I quote, "I have you to tell me every single holiday, but... you can't be writing to me every day of our lives to tell me all the holidays. And, of course, to have a different calendar makes it hard to keep updated every passing year, because it never falls on the same day..." Little did you know that you *would* be stuck with me as your personal Jewish calendar forever!

Well, technology has been developing to our advantage. These days, you can have the Hebrew date displayed alongside the Gregorian date on your Google Calendar really easily.

But hold on a second. What is the Hebrew calendar, anyhow? What are we counting from? Well... tough question, because theoretically, it's supposed to be counting from the creation of the world. That is, it's a calculation using the Bible and the dates and years mentioned in it as a reference. But most modern Orthodox Jews don't actually think the world—or more accurately, the history of homo sapiens, since it's counting from the creation of Adam—is only 5775 years old. We don't think the creation story is meant to be taken literally. The word "Torah" means "instruction." The Torah is an instruction manual, not a history book. So I see it as being more symbolic than anything else; meant to make us reflect on the creation, rather than give a scientific calculation of when it happened. (If you're interested in learning more about how we reconcile science with the Genesis creation story, I highly recommend taking a look at the writings of Dr. Gerald Schroeder, physicist and author of *Genesis and the Big Bang*.)

The names of the Hebrew months (Nisan, Iyar, Sivan, Tamuz, Av, Elul, Tishrei, Cheshvan, Kislev, Tevet, Shvat, Adar) are generally understood to have been adapted from the Babylonian calendar. This makes sense, because our calendar was consolidated, for the most part, during the time of Ezra and Nehemiah, returning from the First Exile in Babylonia. In the Torah, the months are not referred to by names, just "the first month," "the second month," and so forth.

Pop quiz! Which month is the first month of the Hebrew calendar?

...

Trick question!

You know that Rosh Hashana is the Jewish new year, which begins with Tishrei, so you'd think that Tishrei is the first month, right? Not in the Torah. The source for the holiday of Rosh Hashana is Leviticus 23:24: "*In the seventh month, on the first day of the month, shall be a solemn rest unto you, a memorial proclaimed with the blast of horns, a holy convocation.*"

What?

You see, because Jews have a penchant for complicating things, we actually have *four* different new years. The first of Tishrei, otherwise known as Rosh Hashana or the Jewish New Year, is the new year for *years*. That means that we count years from that date, so 5774 turned to 5775 on the first of Tishrei.

The first of Nisan is the new year for *months*. Nisan, not Tishrei, is the first month, and we count the months from there. That's how Tishrei comes out as the seventh month. So when does Nisan fall? Usually around March-April. The first night of Passover falls on the 15th of Nisan.

The other two new years are a little more obscure, so stay with me here.

The first of Elul is the new year for the tithing of cattle. There is a commandment to bring the firstborn of cattle to the Cohanim (priests) and the first of Elul was the start of the "fiscal year" for animals born during that year, similar to how taxes are calculated in countries where the fiscal year starts on a date other than the first of January. This new year is no longer observed, because we no longer have a Temple and the priests cannot receive these offerings. But Elul—which is the month before Tishrei—has taken on the significance of preparing for the High Holidays.

The last of the new years is the 15th of Shvat, or Tu B'Shvat. This new year is used for calculating the age of plants or crops for certain commandments that have to do with agriculture, or for agricultural tithing. It has become known as "the new year for trees," and has become a minor holiday on which we celebrate trees and their fruit. It is customary to eat the new fruit of the season on this day. The Kabbalistic mystics created a sort of ceremony, a "seder" (similar to the Passover Seder) during which they eat symbolic fruit and discuss its significance. It has also evolved into the Israeli Arbor Day, a day to plant new trees and to develop environmental awareness.

So. Why am I telling you all this now?

Because tonight is Rosh Chodesh Shvat, the first day of the new month of Shvat, a month I happen to be especially fond of, not only because I have a thing for trees, but also because my birthday falls on the 3rd.

Birthdays are not much of a big deal in Jewish tradition, though it is said that it's a sign of a righteous person when one dies on one's birthday. (This is said to have been true of Moses and King David.) Generally, important Jewish figures are commemorated on the day of death, not the day of birth. However, we do tend to celebrate like people in many other cultures. We're all about giving thanks on a day that commemorates something good that happened to you, and getting born is pretty high on that list! It is said that on one's birthday, just like on one's wedding day, one has a particularly strong connection to God and can give particularly powerful blessings to others. (The reason for this, by the way, is that such life events bring us joy, and joy brings us closer to God.)

And, well, you've experienced firsthand that my blessings have a fairly good record. If there's something specific you'd like me to pray for this Friday, let me know. Either way, you know I will be (and have been) praying for you.

Chodesh Tov, many blessings, and lots of love,
Daniella

Days of Awe

Dear Josep,

The Hebrew month of Elul is just around the corner, and I have to say, it is my favorite time of year.

There is something magical in the air toward the end of the scorching Middle Eastern summer, when a cool breeze wafts in and big, puffy clouds start to appear on the horizon, softening the once-brutal sun. Sometimes those clouds even bring with them a few drops of promise-rain. The sky, almost white during the end of summer from the dust in the air, clears to a deeper blue. The squill, a tall pyramidal flower with small white blossoms, pops up suddenly from the brittle brown of the sun-dried grasses. This flower, known in Hebrew as the *chatzav*, is the harbinger of autumn in Israel. And then there are the pomegranates. I never saw pomegranate trees growing along the coast where I spent my first decade in Israel, but here in Judea they grow wild and you can see them ripening during Elul. Best of all, you can buy massive amounts of them and stain your fingers to your heart's content with their crimson juice, because they become the cheapest fruit by the kilo at our local supermarket when they're in season. Nothing says Elul and Tishrei like the tangy sweetness of pomegranate.

Days of Awe

Starting before sunrise on the first day of Elul and continuing every morning until Yom Kippur, the Sephardi and Mizrachi men gather in the synagogue to recite *selichot*, the special prayers in the days preceding the High Holidays asking God for forgiveness. During the services, the rousing call of the shofar—the ram's horn—carries into the streets from the synagogues. Throngs of tourists, most of them Israeli, flood to the old neighborhoods in the ancient cities of Jerusalem and Safed for "selichot tours," visiting the many synagogues there with their different traditions, prayers, and melodies. Ashkenazim begin to recite selichot the Saturday night preceding Rosh Hashana, or, if Rosh Hashana falls in the first half of the week, the Saturday night before that one.

Elul is a month of introspection, reflection, soul searching, prayer, and forgiveness. The Sages say that this month, "The King is in the field." If God is compared to a king in a palace, where most of the time, it takes many hurdles and obstacles and bureaucracy to gain an audience with Him, during Elul it is as if He has flung open the palace gates and walked out toward you in the field. This allegory means that it is a time of particular spiritual closeness to God.

I loved this time of year in high school. You know me, I'm a "soul archeologist" by nature and introspection is one of my favorite pastimes—sometimes to a fault!—so I especially loved activities geared toward making us think about spirituality and our relationships with God. They'd invite people, often Jews who used to be secular and went through a process of becoming religious, who would speak to us about their spiritual journey of *teshuva* (return to their spiritual roots). We would have concerts of soft spiritual music, and that music would stir awake the yearning for God that we often ignore. I have several memories of lying on the grass somewhere, looking up at a sky full of stars, singing softly, with tears pouring down my face, just feeling that strange mingling of an unquenchable yearning with an overwhelming sense of being loved by Him.

These days I don't have evenings of spiritual music built into my curriculum, but I do have those clouds, that sky, that gentle breeze, and the sound of the shofar echoing from the Sephardi synagogue near my home.

The Ten Days of Repentance

I will elaborate on the Jewish concept of repentance, teshuva, later in the book.[26] The first ten days of the month of Tishrei focus on teshuva as a national, collective process. The reason for this is that on Rosh Hashana—the Jewish new year, the first two days of Tishrei—it is believed that God figuratively "opens the books" and sets down all the decrees for the coming year, based on what we merit, deserve, and need according to our deeds from the previous year. However, tradition has it, on Rosh Hashana God does not "seal" our fates—He merely "writes them down," and does not seal them until the end of the tenth of Tishrei, which is Yom Kippur, literally "the Day of Atonement." So during the ten days between lighting the candles of Rosh Hashana and the final shofar blast of Yom Kippur, we have the power to change those decrees, through teshuva, giving charity, and prayer.

Now, as you will see in the letter about teshuva, on an individual level, we can change the spiritual influence of our sins at any time during the year. So the question arises: why do we need the Ten Days of Repentance? What does it mean that the decrees are "written" and "sealed"? The answer is that the Ten Days of Repentance are not really about individual teshuva, though they are an opportune time to focus on it. They're about teshuva as a community, as a collective. We're not really coming together on Rosh Hashana and Yom Kippur to pray for ourselves as individuals, nor for just ourselves as a community; we come together to pray for *the entire universe*.

Rosh Hashana is the Jewish new year because it is believed to be "the birthday of the world." But it isn't actually the day we believe the world was created. It is the day we believe that *humans* were created. That is, the sixth day of creation, not the

---

[26] See: *Teshuva: As Long as the Candle Burns*.

first. So why do we count starting from Adam's birthday, and not from the day God said, "Let there be light"?

It is because the Torah's focus is on humans and our role in elevating the universe spiritually. It is really all about us. The famous Hassidic rebbe, Rabbi Simcha Bunem, taught his students that they should carry two notes, one in each pocket, at all times. One note should read, "The world was created for me," and the other should read, "And I am dust and ashes." The idea is that, on the one hand, we should remember the greatness of the role and responsibility for which we were created; and on the other hand, we must remember that we are made of dust and will return to dust, and must balance that responsibility with humility.

As Jews, our responsibility is that much greater, in that we believe God gave us a unique and crucial role in the process of spiritually elevating the universe. And during the Ten Days of Repentance, the weight of that responsibility is heavy. God asked us to be a light unto the nations, to spread knowledge of Him throughout the world, to abolish injustice and evil. And when we stand before Him on the day the world is judged, we have to answer for ourselves and what we have done, as a nation, in the past year, to further that goal.

That is why the High Holidays (Rosh Hashana and Yom Kippur) are often seen as being very grave and serious holidays. They are also known as the Days of Awe. But they are also filled with joy, singing, celebration, and a strong sense of community.

Rosh Hashana

Rosh Hashana is a *Yom Tov*. Yom Tov literally means "good day" and it applies to holidays that are listed in the Torah (the first five books of the Bible). What it means in practice is that it is a holiday that is celebrated very similarly to how we celebrate Shabbat; we light candles at the beginning and make Havdalah at the end, have festive prayers, eat two feasts (one at night and one during the day), and observe almost the same restrictions (barring certain activities that are related to preparing food). Now, in most cases, there's a difference between the duration of the holiday depending on whether you are in Israel or outside it. Inside Israel, a Yom Tov lasts one day. Outside of it, it lasts two. The reason is this: before we had calendars, Jews would calculate the months and the holidays according to observations of the moon. A month in the Jewish calendar, you see, can sometimes be twenty-nine days, and sometimes thirty. A witness for the Sanhedrin, the great rabbinical assembly, would have to sight the new moon and announce it to the rest of the nation. If you lived in Israel at the time, chances were that by the time the 15th of the month came around (which is when most Jewish holidays fall) you would have heard from these witnesses and would have an accurate calculation of the beginning of the month. If you lived outside of Israel, however, the news might not reach you by then. So Jews in the Diaspora observed two days of Yom Tov, just in case they had miscalculated and the holiday actually fell a day later than they thought.

In the case of Rosh Hashana, however, the holiday falls on the very first day of the month, and there was concern that even those in Israel would miscalculate. Therefore, even in Israel, we observe two days of Rosh Hashana instead of one.

Due to the intensity and significance of the High Holidays, the prayer services during Rosh Hashana and Yom Kippur are particularly long. There are so many additional prayers that we have special prayer books only for the High Holidays, called *machzorim*, literally "cycles." If a normal Shabbat morning service runs from 8:00-10:30, Rosh Hashana services will easily run until 1pm, depending on the congregation, how fast the cantor goes, how much singing there is, etc.

The Shofar

One thing that is unique about the Rosh Hashana services is the blowing of the shofar.

A shofar is a hollowed out horn of a kosher animal that is blown like a musical horn. It was used as a call to battle during Biblical times, and features in the story of how Joshua defeated Jericho. It symbolizes the ram that was sacrificed in place of Isaac, and its purpose is to "awaken" our souls to repent.

My most poignant experience of hearing the shofar blown was actually not on Rosh Hashana at all. It was in the Łopuchowo Forest in Poland. (I write more about my trip to Poland in *In the Empty Synagogues of Poland* later on.) We were standing over a mass grave there, where all the residents of the town of Tykocin were murdered by the Nazis. After a small ceremony we held in their memory, the principal of my school stood in front of us. "There are things," he said, "that are so raw, so powerful, so great, that they can't be expressed in words. Sometimes the only way to express how you feel is to cry out from the depths of your soul. And sometimes, even the human voice is not enough to give expression to this cry." He reached into his bag and took out a shofar. "When I blow this shofar," he said, "let it be your voice." He blew it, and there wasn't a dry eye in the crowd. Since that day, every time I hear the shofar, I'm transported back to that moment in the Łopuchowo Forest, with my soul crying out in pain, in yearning, in hope.

That is the idea of the shofar. It gives a voice to the deepest cries of our souls.

A Sweet New Year

Now, as with all Jewish holidays, food has a significant role in the celebrations! As I mentioned, there are two feasts, one during the evening and one during the day. Like on Shabbat, the meals are preceded by Kiddush over wine and a blessing over two loaves of bread. On Rosh Hashana, round loaves of bread are served, symbolizing the cycle of the year. Additionally, there is a custom to dip the bread in honey, as a sign that we are wishing for a "sweet" new year. We take this further with the iconic, symbolic food eaten on Rosh Hashana: apples dipped in honey. The apples, which are round, also symbolize the year.

Many also have the custom to eat other symbolic foods, whose Hebrew names are reminiscent of other things we wish for. One of the most widely eaten of these symbolic foods is pomegranates. As I mentioned, the pomegranates are just starting to ripen. They are one of the Seven Species,[27] and my personal favorite fruit. Their many seeds are symbolic of prosperity and fertility—and the Torah. You see, if you ever sat down and counted all the seeds in a pomegranate, you would discover that the number of seeds comes out astonishingly close to 613—the number of *mitzvot*, commandments in the Torah. When we eat pomegranate on Rosh Hashana, we say, "*May it be Your will, our God and God of our forefathers, that our merits be as numerous as [the seeds of] a pomegranate.*" I don't know if this is a widely accepted idea, but I also think the little "crown" at the top of the fruit is symbolic of one of the themes of Rosh Hashana: proclaiming God's kingship over the universe.

Yom Kippur

Yom Kippur is the climax of the Ten Days of Repentance. Tradition has it that this is the day the fate of the world in the coming year is sealed. Thus, it is the holiest day of the Jewish year, the "Sabbath of Sabbaths."

I constantly emphasize that Judaism is about life in this world, about elevating the mundane and channeling our base desires for a higher spiritual purpose. Yom Kippur is the only day of the Jewish year on which we deny ourselves worldly pleasures rather than use them as part of our service of God and spiritual refinement. It is the day we try to be like the angels, which, in Jewish thought, are messengers of God or channels through which He manifests His will in the physical

---

[27] See *Blessings: Finding God in an Apple*, under *Blessings of Enjoyment*.

world, and thus have no will of their own. Many of us wear white clothing to symbolize purity from sin.

The restrictions of Yom Kippur are the same as Shabbat, with the added restrictions of a major fast day, which include eating, drinking, wearing leather shoes, washing, anointing ourselves with oil, and marital relations.[28] Not much left to do, then, except pray! And pray we do. Yom Kippur is the only day in the Jewish year with five prayer services: one in the evening (Ma'ariv), one in the morning (Shacharit), one right after Shacharit (Musaf), one in the afternoon (Mincha), and one just at the end of the fast, called *Ne'ila*, which means "locking," as in the "locking of the gates of prayer."

The first prayer of Yom Kippur is the famous Kol Nidre. Well, actually it's not so much a prayer as a kind of juristic declaration that annuls all vows taken in the last year (the ones you take upon yourself, not ones that involve other people) and declares it permissible to pray with outcasts and sinners. The origin of the formula is unknown, but it's believed to have been created during the Geonic period (the last half of the first millennium C.E.) during a time of extreme persecution where many Jews were forcibly converted to Christianity or Islam. The common theory is that the idea of the passage was to welcome such Jews back into the fold and declare their conversions to those other religions null and void.

One would imagine that it was a very important prayer to crypto-Jews during the time of the Spanish Inquisition. There are those who theorize that the haunting melody most commonly sung has its origins in pre-expulsion Spain. It is certainly reminiscent of the *saetas* in Andalusia during Holy Week.

The evening continues with the reading of the Thirteen Attributes of Mercy, a formula God gave Moses when he was pleading that God forgive the Israelites for the sin of the Golden Calf. There are a number of powerful liturgical poems that are sung. One of my favorites is *Ki Hinei KaChomer*, "Like

---

[28] See *Starving for God: Jewish Fast Days* for more on major vs. minor fast days.

Clay": "*For like clay in the potter's hand/With his will, he expands it, and with his will, contracts it/So are we in Your hand, Rememberer of Kindness/Look to the Covenant, and disregard the evil inclination...*"

Selichot are also said, as well as the usual Amidah prayer for the High Holidays. There is also an added passage of confession: a double acrostic poem of all different kinds of sins, written in first person plural. "*For the sin we have committed before You under duress or willingly... for the sin we have committed before You by hard-heartedness...*" Through speech, or through deceit, or through disrespect, or inadvertently—"*And for them all, God of pardon, pardon us, forgive us, atone for us.*"

The morning services are also full of beautiful prayers and poems. If you ever get a chance to flip through a High Holiday machzor, I highly recommend it.

It's really hard to describe the experience of the prayers of Yom Kippur. There is an intense sense of connectedness, both with the community, and with God; a sense of standing barehearted before the King of Kings, and saying, "I know I haven't been all I could be, and I want to be better." I used to say that Yom Kippur was my favorite holiday because it was the day I felt closest to God. These days, between fasting and taking care of little kids, it's much harder to connect in that way. But even so, even if I manage to spend just a little time in synagogue, or take the time to say some of my favorite Yom Kippur prayers... it feels like peeling away the layers of my soul, one by one, sometimes painfully, to touch the Divine core of my being, and connect with He from whom that core originates. Because, you see, Yom Kippur really is the cleansing of our souls from the soil of sin, of doubt, of fear, of distance from God, and from ourselves and what we want to be. That may sound awfully abstract and "out there"... but I think you, of all people, will get it.

When the fast is over, traditionally, the first thing we do (after guzzling water and stuffing our faces with cake, of course) is start building the *succah*, because that is the major mitzvah of the next holiday that comes up only five days later, and we want to act on our freshly renewed commitment to our covenant with God, and get the year off to a good start with our shiny, clean souls.

Wishing a meaningful Elul full of self-discovery and renewal to all of us, and may we be written and sealed in the Book of Life.

Love,
Daniella

In God's Presence: Succot & Shmini Atzeret

Dear Josep,

So after all the intense action of the first ten days of Tishrei, you'd think God would give us a nice break for the rest of the month.

Nope.

The night after Yom Kippur, the banging of hammers and clinking of metal rods begins to sound throughout the Jewish neighborhoods.

And very soon, strange little booths begin to pop up in yards and on balconies—some with metal frames and walls of cloth; some made of wood; some covered with palm branches, some in bamboo mats. The children bring home a pile of paper chains, mobiles, and other decorations from school. And this morning we woke up, all partied out from Shabbat (and Yom Kippur, Shabbat, and the two days of Rosh Hashana in the past two weeks...) to face yet *another* Jewish holiday.

Succot is one of the lesser-known, yet nonetheless important Jewish holidays. "Succot" means "booths" and the holiday is called that because the main commandment of the holiday is to build an impermanent structure—a succah—outside our homes, and basically live in it for seven days.

In God's Presence

Okay, so what on earth is this about? I mean, we've got the other two *Regalim*, Passover and Shavuot, and each one commemorates a very important event in the forming of the Jewish nation. What happened on the 15th of Tishrei that involved moving out of our homes into a booth?

Well, nothing actually happened on the 15th of Tishrei. But while Passover commemorates the Exodus, and Shavuot commemorates the giving of the Torah, Succot commemorates something else, something less momentous, and more subtle, but nonetheless crucial to our daily lives. The succot represent the Clouds of Glory that surrounded the Israelites as they walked through the desert from Egypt to the Promised Land. In the text of the Torah, it says that the Israelites were led through the desert by a pillar of cloud during the day and a pillar of fire during the night. The Sages teach us that they were actually surrounded by this protective cloud on all sides: above, to protect from the brutal desert sun; below, to protect them from scorpions and snakes; and on all sides, to protect them from bandits and wild animals.

So what makes me say that is this so relevant to our daily lives?

Because this holiday is really about understanding that, like fish who can't see the water in which they swim, we're constantly immersed in God's presence. After a month and a half of introspection, breaking down the barriers between us and God and between ourselves and who we want to be, the time has come to simply bask in God's glory and remind ourselves that He is always with us.

So for seven days, we move out of the comfort and security of our permanent homes, into these little impermanent structures. While they represent the Clouds of Glory protecting us, they also represent the impermanence of this physical world. And in the typical style of Judaism, we focus our attention and our lives on our existence within that world, celebrating all the goodness God has given us within it.

As usual in Jewish law, there are strict specifications for what qualifies as a succah. It must have at least two and a half walls that are at least 80 cm high and do not move around too much in the wind. The interior must measure at least 56cm by 56cm. Its roof must be made out of organic material—branches or leaves that are disconnected from their source—and parts of the succah that are covered by a permanent roof or a living tree do not qualify. The branches or leaves must be sparse enough so that the rain can come through and the stars are visible through them. The idea is that, though it's impermanent, and insecure, and at the mercy of the elements, we fear no evil, for God is with us.

Succot begins with a Yom Tov (or two outside Israel, as explained in the letter on the Days of Awe). Then follow six days of *chol hamo'ed*, "the mundane of the holiday," during which we are not restricted from all the acts of creation like on Shabbat and Yom Tov, but are supposed to refrain from working as much as we can. During these seven (or eight) days, we must eat all our meals in the succah, and sleep in it if possible. It is strongly encouraged—as always—to host guests in one's *succah*, and there is a Kabbalistic concept that a special spiritual "guest" comes to "visit" us for each day of the holiday: Abraham the first day, Isaac the second, then Jacob, Joseph, Moses, Aaron, and finally David. We call them *"ushpizin"* (Aramaic for "guests") and recite a special passage "inviting" them in (or, more accurately, the spiritual attribute each of them represent—which correspond to the Kabbalistic spheres as I explain later in *Counting Up: The Omer & Lag B'Omer*).

The other special commandment of Succot is "taking the four species."

The Four Species

When I was collecting ideas for a post on "weird things Jews do," this one came up a lot, but I left it out of that list because it's not just a weird habit or tradition—it's an actual mitzvah, a Torah commandment.

So what are the four species?

Think Palm Sunday on steroids.[29]

Leviticus 23:40: *"And you shall take for yourselves on the first day, the fruit of the citrus tree, date palm fronds, a branch of a braided tree, and willows of the brook, and you shall rejoice before the Lord your God for a seven day period."*

These are the *lulav* and *etrog*. The lulav is a cluster of three types of branches: a date palm frond in the center (also called a lulav), three myrtle branches on the right (*hadassim*), and two willow branches (*aravot*) on the left. The etrog is a citron (*el poncem* for you), a lemon-like citrus fruit with a thick rind. Together, they comprise the *arba minim*, the four species.

So, um... what do we do with them?

While we pray during the holiday, we hold them together, and at specified points in the prayers, shake them in all directions, the lulav in the right hand, and the etrog in the left, opposite the heart. The idea is, again, to remind us of God's presence all around us.

Now, for anybody (with the possible exception of a religious Christian!), this makes for a pretty bizarre-looking scene: a bunch of guys parading around the synagogue holding a clump of plants and chanting.

So what's the symbolism here? Why these plants?

The two most common explanations are as follows: one states that plants symbolize the different parts of the body. The etrog represents the heart; the lulav, the spine; the myrtle, the eyes, and the willow, the mouth (each because of the shape of their leaves). The idea is that we are subjugating all these parts of our bodies—our hearts and minds, our limbs, our eyes and power of sight, and our mouths and power of speech—to service of God. The other explanation is that the plants symbolize four different kinds of Jews. The etrog, which

---

[29] For the Jews, Muslims or otherwise uninformed among you: Palm Sunday is the Sunday before Easter, and in many traditions, it is celebrated by holding a procession of the congregants carrying palm fronds, in commemoration of Jesus's triumphal entry into Jerusalem before the crucifixion.

has a fragrance and a flavor, represents a Jew who studies Torah and performs good deeds. The date palm, which has flavor, but no fragrance, represents one who performs good deeds, but does not study Torah. The myrtle, which has fragrance but no flavor, represents the opposite; and the willow, which has neither fragrance nor flavor, represents a Jew who does neither. We are to strive to be like the etrog.

So the four species symbolize the different components of who we are, as individuals and as a community. And the idea of holding and shaking them during the prayers is that during this particular celebration of God's presence, we're coming together and devoting everything we are to the continuous pursuit of His closeness. We seek Him in our diverse community, in our words, in our deeds, in our thoughts, and in our hearts.

Shmini Atzeret & Simchat Torah

So you'd think that after the intense first ten days of the month of Tishrei *and* the seven or eight days of Succot, then we would finally get a break!

Nope.

Often lumped together with Succot, the Yom Tov that follows immediately after its conclusion is not actually part of Succot, but a separate holiday in its own right. We do not eat in the succah on this day, and it doesn't have any unique commandments of its own. The name Shmini Atzeret means something like "the final eighth day." It's kind of like the "after-party" of the Tishrei Holiday extravaganza. You know how it's like one in the morning and you just finished a lovely meal with your new friends from the USA and Israel, and the one from Israel is going to be flying home in the morning and you don't know when you'll ever see her again, and you've had such a lovely time getting to know each other and getting back to your normal routine is going to be so depressing... so you suggest going to hang out at a pub on La Rambla, to spend just a little more time together? Like that...

But because there's no specific commandment associated with Shmini Atzeret, the Sages decided to designate it as the holiday to celebrate renewing the cycle of the weekly Torah portions. You see, the Torah (as in the first five books of the Bible) is divided into portions, and a different one is read each week. It takes a year to get through all the portions, and Shmini Atzeret is when we read the last portion and celebrate the completion of the Torah readings. For that reason, it is also called Simchat Torah, "rejoicing in the Torah."

I should point out that they are only on the same day in Israel. Outside of Israel, because of the need for two days of Yom Tov (explained in *Days of Awe*), they are split. The first day is Shmini Atzeret, and the second day, Simchat Torah.

So what does celebrating the completion of the Torah readings involve? A whole lot of dancing and singing! The congregation takes out all the Torah scrolls and dances with them, shoving all the chairs and benches in the synagogue to the side. This part of the services can last for hours on Simchat Torah, and it occurs both during the evening services and the morning services. Parents involve the children by dancing with them (fathers often put their kids on their shoulders) and candy is frequently distributed.

In the morning, after all the dancing, the last portion of the Torah is read, followed by the beginning of the first portion of Genesis, kind of like how you finish a really great book and you can't help but just start it all over again right away! (Okay, actually, it's exactly that.)

And *then*... we finally get a break! The month after Tishrei, Cheshvan, is devoid of holidays, and the holiday in the following month is at the end of it (the 25th of Kislev is Chanukah). Other than finally getting back to our normal routines, we use this time to focus on praying for rain, as the rainy season in Israel begins at this time. And that, my friend, is a topic for another letter.

Love,
Daniella

Let There Be Light

---◆---

Dear Josep,
Chanukah is the most famous of Jewish holidays. But it is actually a minor rabbinical holiday, of less importance than most of the other Jewish holidays. So why is it so well-known, you wonder?
One word: Christmas.
Many cultures have a holiday around this time of year. Skeptics would say this is a remnant of ancient pagan celebrations of the winter solstice. I would say, there is something about this time of year that people are drawn to. When the darkness is greatest, we are most compelled to search for the light.
So what is the darkness that the Jews encountered that compelled us to find the light of Chanukah?
You've probably heard the story before, so I'll be brief: the story of Chanukah goes that during the Hellenistic period, the Greek ruler over Judea made laws that were increasingly anti-Jewish and oppressive, banning circumcision and kosher slaughter, institutionalizing idol worship, and defiling the Holy Temple. A motley band of Jewish fighters—the Maccabees—rebelled against the Greeks, and in a series of miraculous battles, won back Jewish sovereignty over the land and

Let There Be Light

over Jerusalem, and were able to restore the Temple and rededicate it to the service of God. (The word "Chanukah," חנוכה, means "rededication.") But, the story goes, there was one problem: when searching for pure oil to use to light the Menorah, the seven-branched candelabra that burned constantly in the Temple, they were only able to find one small bottle—enough oil to burn for one day. It would take eight days to acquire a new supply of pure oil. The miracle of Chanukah is that after they lit the Menorah, expecting it to go out after one day... it burned, and burned, and burned, for all eight days. That's why we light the nine-branched *chanukiyah* for Chanukah—one candle for each day, and one with which to light the others. We start with one candle on the first day, and add a candle every night until there are eight.

On the surface, we've got a nice David and Goliath style story here of an unlikely military victory, plus a nice little miracle that has to do with a lamp. But what is the real light here, and what is the real darkness? Is the darkness the oppression of the Greeks, and the light, the light of the Menorah in the Temple? Or is there something else to this story?

Let's zoom in a little on the period before the Maccabees. If you were picturing the Jews looking on in horror while the Greeks went about their hedonistic shenanigans, think again. As you full well know, Greek culture was not just about oppressing Jews—it was an incredibly powerful and advanced culture, with superior science, philosophy, and technology, and there was a lot that was attractive about it. Western culture as we know it today is built on the marriage between the Greek culture and Judeo-Christian values. And Jews have always liked to be on top of the latest and greatest progress in the world. So many, many Jews embraced the Greek culture and adopted it as their own—and began to shed their Jewishness. They agreed with the Greeks, who scorned Judaism as being primitive, backwards, and irrelevant. It was time to move forward in the world and become part of real progress, instead of clinging to their tragic past and the covenant with God that their forefathers had broken.

Does this sound familiar in any way...?

If I asked you what the greatest danger to Judaism is and has been throughout history, you might answer oppression, hatred, and antisemitism. I beg to differ. The greatest danger to Judaism is assimilation.

Assimilation means losing sight of what it is that makes us special. It means losing sight of our purpose, our essence, our unique contribution to the world. It means allowing our unique voice to be swallowed up into the cacophony and confusion of humanity's global conversation. Assimilation is darkness.

God said, "Let there be light."

We believe that God created humans to elevate the world to a higher spiritual place. And we believe that God chose us as a nation to guide our fellow humans to that place. To be a "light unto the nations."

See where I'm going with this?

The real darkness in the story of Chanukah was not the external force of the Greeks' oppression; the real darkness was **doubt**. Doubt that our identity, our message, our traditions had anything to say to the Greeks, doubt that they had importance in the grand scheme of things. And the light was more than just the Menorah that quietly burned eight times as long as it should have. The light was the essence of the Jewish people, which has survived a hundred times longer than it should have, which has refused to be extinguished despite the sound and fury of hundreds of cultures that swept the world, only to fade over time. But our light never faded. It burned, and burned, and burned. And in the midst of it all, the Torah is the "candle for our feet, the light to our path" (to slightly paraphrase Psalms 119:105), whispering in our ears the truth that God spoke to us at Mount Sinai. The Torah is the pillar of fire that continues to lead us through the desert to the Promised Land.

And as more and more Jews see no reason to hold on to the faith of their ancestors, and their children and grandchildren lose all connection to that past, it is more important than ever to emphasize this message of Chanukah: *There is something special about you and the people you come from. Something that God gave you, making you who you are and giving you the unique mission only you can complete. That is your light.* **Own it.**

On that note... I wish you a holiday, and indeed a life, full of light, full of the truth within you. And I pray that you will never be afraid to own your light, and let it shine on everyone around you.

Much love,
Daniella

Purim:
Divine Hide-and-Seek

Dear Josep,

I don't know what gave you the impression that dressing up in costumes is a thing we do for every holiday. Eitan was correct, it really is only for Purim! Could be that you got that impression because I was particularly fond of that tradition and used it as an outlet for my theatrical silliness... hence the Hassidic Jack Sparrow.[30] I used to take the opportunity to express some personal joke from that year. But I guess my life has become more boring as I got older, because my costumes have gotten simpler and tamer, and I'm out of personal jokes for costume ideas. This year my oldest decided to dress up as Darth Vader (don't ask me why... I think he saw someone with that costume last year) so I'm going along with the theme as Princess Leia. (I told Eitan he should be Chewbacca. He was not amused.)

Anyway, let me set you straight: the common denominator in Jewish holidays is not costumes, it is **food**. There's a joke that all Jewish holidays follow the same theme: "They tried to kill us, we won, let's eat!" It's true for *almost* all of the holidays, and Purim is no exception. Much as we joke about it, it really is reflected solidly in halakha: every celebration is marked with

---

[30] Don't even ask, dear reader. Don't. Even. Ask.

at least one festive meal, including most holidays, weddings, and circumcisions. It's one expression of the concept of channeling the material world to bring us to greater spiritual heights. We use the worldly pleasures and enjoyment to help us connect to the spiritual.

So, Purim! The holiday commemorates the story of Queen Esther and the Jews of Persia, which is recounted in the Book of Esther in the Bible. Long story short, an evil guy named Haman convinced the King of Persia (Xerxes, or in Hebrew, Achashverosh) to issue a decree stating that all the Jews in the empire were to be killed on the 13th of the month of Adar, 356 B.C.E. It just so happened that the woman recently selected as queen, Esther, was secretly Jewish, and with the aid of her wise uncle, Mordekhai, she turned the tables on Haman and saved the Jews. Long story *very* short... repeat after me... "They tried to kill us, we won, let's eat!"

The remarkable thing about the Book of Esther is that even though it's clearly a story of God rescuing the Jews from a terrible fate (as per usual) it doesn't mention God's name even once. One might think that it was Esther's actions that saved the Jews, or her Uncle Mordekhai's advice. One might even go so far as to argue that it was all just a bunch of lucky coincidences—the right people being in the right place at the right time. "Purim" means "lots," in commemoration of the lottery Haman cast to decide which date to designate as "Kill the Jews Day." So even the name of the holiday implies chance, not Divine intervention.

But we know that there's no such thing as coincidence. And that's the main theme of Purim: *Things are not what they seem*. This is where the tradition of dressing in costumes comes from—as well as the tradition of eating foods that have some kind of "hidden" element in them. The most famous of these is hamentaschen, little triangle-shaped cookies stuffed with a sweet filling.

Purim is a celebration of the Divine game of hide-and-seek; of God "hiding" himself in the mundane, behind science, behind history, behind strong and charismatic people, and waiting for you to recognize Him behind these disguises.

Purim is also about Jewish unity. One of the things the "bad guy," Haman, says to King Achashverosh about the Jews is that they are "scattered and separate among all the nations." (Esther 3:8). We strive to counter that "separateness" Haman noted, by expressing our unity and love for one another, by giving charity, sending food to one another, and having a big feast with our friends and family. These things are not just recommendations or traditions; they are mitzvot, commandments, **required** by Jewish law on Purim day. Most people send each other gift baskets, usually of sweets.

The other commandment of Purim is to hear Megillat Esther (the Scroll of Esther) cantillated aloud in the synagogue both night and day. Since the obligation to hear the Megillah is equal for men and women (unlike the obligation to hear the Torah, which is only for men), women can read the Megillah for themselves, and in my community we have a reading by women for women. I learned how to cantillate from the Torah and Megillah from my mother, and I usually participate in these readings.

Purim being a very joyful holiday, it's traditional to get drunk during the feast... but I'm not a fan. I never particularly liked drinking. I'll enjoy the occasional wine or sweet liquor, but only a little. The only time I ever got drunk, I was eighteen months old. Yes, I said months. But that's a story for another time!

In most of the world, Purim is celebrated on the 14th of Adar. However, according to the Scroll of Esther, the war between the Jews and their enemies continued in the walled cities, such as Shushan, into the 15th. That's why, the scroll explains, Jews in "walled cities" celebrate a day later. However, the Sages did not want to honor a foreign city more than our holy city Jerusalem, which lay desolate when the miracle of Purim occurred. Therefore, they decided that the distinction of "walled city" would be granted to any city that was walled during the time of the conquest of Joshua. The only city that falls under this category for certain is Jerusalem, but there are other ancient cities in Israel, such as Jaffa, Akko, Hebron, Safed, and Tiberius, which may have been walled at that time. So there is a custom in those places to hold a second Megillah reading on the 15th—just in case.

A joyful Purim to you and yours!

Love,
Daniella

Passover, Part I: Freedom, Education, and National Obsessive-Compulsive Disorder

Dear Josep,

So I figured out why I never sent you an e-mail specifically about Passover, even back in 2007 when I would get concerned notes from you wondering if something was wrong because you hadn't heard from me in five days.

(... Yes, apparently that happened.)

(... Twice.)

The reason is that it's just not possible to capture Passover in a single e-mail. No, not even a Daniella Standard Size e-mail.

So I'm splitting this topic into two parts. In Part I, I'll discuss the general concepts of the holiday. In Part II, I'll go into detail about the Seder night and the Haggadah.

To begin, let's turn to the old template for most Jewish holidays: "They tried to kill us, we won, let's eat!" Does it apply here? Why, yes it does!

As you probably know, Passover is the celebration commemorating our freedom from slavery in Egypt, also known as the Exodus.

It begins on the 15th of Nisan, which is the day the Israelites left Egypt, and lasts seven days in Israel, eight outside Israel. It is one of the three Regalim holidays mentioned in the

Torah, on which we were required to make a pilgrimage to the Temple in Jerusalem. (*Regel* means "foot.")[31]

The first night (or two nights outside of Israel) is the crux of the holiday: the Seder night. You may have heard of the Seder. It is believed to have been Jesus's "last supper" (hence the proximity to Easter). As mentioned, we will elaborate on the Seder in Part II.

But first: why is the Exodus such an important event in the history of our people?

There's a vast amount of rabbinic literature that addresses this question, but here's the simple answer: the Exodus marks the birth of the nation of Israel. The narrative of the Bible, up until that point, follows a number of individuals, or at most a family, and their interactions with God. We became a multitude under slavery; we became a nation, with a destiny and a purpose, when God gave us our freedom.

It is said that God wanted us to be slaves before giving us the Torah to develop our sense of empathy and justice. You can never really understand someone until you've experienced his pain. And you can never know and appreciate the true value of freedom if you've never been a slave. Our purpose is to be a "light unto the nations," to spread kindness, compassion, and justice throughout a corrupt world. We couldn't have done this without first knowing pain, cruelty, and injustice.

The goal of the Seder night is for every one of us to relive the experience of being freed from slavery. It is a multi-sensory, hands-on, educational production, and it revolves around passing the message to the next generation. As we've discussed, educating children is a very important mitzvah, and the purpose of some of the strange customs on Seder night is to provoke the children to ask questions. Raising questions is a classic Jewish educational method. We even tend to like excellent questions better than we like excellent answers.

---

[31] For more about the Three Regalim and the discrepancy between the duration of holidays depending on location, see *Days of Awe* and *In God's Presence: Succot & Shmini Atzeret*.

So, that's freedom, and education. National obsessive-compulsive disorder?!

Well... yeah. This is another thing that makes Passover so special, and also such a pain in the neck. Over the seven days of Passover, we're not allowed to eat or possess *chametz*. "Chametz" means leavened products. That is, any product made out of grain (wheat, barley, oats, spelt, or rye) and water that was cooked for more than eighteen minutes after the flour came in contact with the water—therefore beginning the process of fermentation that causes the dough to rise and become puffy.

Um... wait, you say. Is there *any* type of grain product that is baked in under eighteen minutes?!

Why, yes, there is. It's called... matzah.

Matzah is the bread of Passover, referred to in the Haggadah as the "bread of affliction." Apt, because it looks and tastes like cardboard, and we're required to eat a fair amount of it on Seder night. (Okay, okay, it's not that bad. It's like a very plain cracker.)

So what's the problem with leavened bread?

(Good, good, keep up the questions!)

The practical answer is that the Israelites were granted their freedom very quickly and they had no time to get ready for their trip out of Egypt. The Torah says that they didn't have time to let their dough rise for bread, so they made *matzot* to take on their journey. The prohibition against eating chametz, and the mitzvah of eating matzah, are both in commemoration of that. There's also an idea that chametz represents the ego, and that on Passover we clean it out of our homes and souls.

So the thing is, you know how obsessive-compulsive Jewish law is about things we're not allowed to eat... and this applies to chametz, too. In fact, it is even *more* strict than the laws of kashrut. This means that we have to literally kasher our kitchens before the holiday. (This, as I've been trying to tell you all these years, is not nearly as fun as you think it is!) Most of us have an entirely different set of dishes and cookware set aside specifically for Passover, because not everything can be kashered, and because, again, kashering pots and pans can be a serious pain.

We're also not allowed to *own* any chametz, which means we have to clean our houses thoroughly (especially us parents of toddlers) to make sure no bits of crackers/cereal/bread are in accessible places. People (by which I mean "crazy Jewish housewives") often take this to the extreme and use it as an opportunity to do a very thorough spring clean... but much of this isn't really necessary.

The prohibition against eating chametz also gave way to the most famous of legal fictions in Jewish law. Obviously, getting rid of all one's chametz can be impractical at best and financially damaging at worst, especially for stores and factories. So we have a rather silly solution: we "sell" the chametz to a non-Jew during the seven days of Passover, keep it covered/hidden during the holiday, and "buy" it back afterwards.

... By the way, can I interest you in some instant oatmeal and maybe a few pitas?

(I kid, I kid. These days we can sell our chametz very easily through rabbis who centralize the "sales" and sell them to a designated non-Jew. We can do this through our synagogue or even on the Internet.)

Well, that's Passover in a nutshell. Stay tuned for Part II, in which we'll discuss the details of the aforementioned multisensory, hands-on, educational production we call the Seder.

Love,
Daniella

Passover, Part II: Seder Night 101

Dear Josep,

In Part I, I mentioned that the Seder (and Passover in general) are all about interactive and experiential learning that's usually directed toward the next generation: the kids. This actually does not begin on Seder night, but on the night before, with a special ritual we call *bedikat chametz*.

Bedikat Chametz

In the weeks and days before Passover, as mentioned in Part I, we thoroughly clean and check our homes for any recognizable traces of chametz (leavened products; see Part I for explanation). On the evening before Passover, we hold a special ritual to symbolically finish this task, called bedikat chametz, "checking for chametz." We make a blessing, and then turn off all the lights in the house, and by the light of candles and flashlights, search for little pieces of chametz that were intentionally hidden by one of the family members (traditionally, it's ten pieces). Obviously, this would be an extremely inefficient way to *actually* check for chametz. It's more symbolic than anything else, and it's a fun game for the kids, kind of like a treasure hunt in the dark! When all the pieces of chametz have been found, we recite a passage in Aramaic that effectively nullifies any chametz that we have missed in our search. We declare that if there is any chametz left, to us it will be like "the dust of the earth."

The following day, any remaining chametz (that will not be sold) must be burned or otherwise destroyed in a way that makes it unusable, such as pouring bleach all over it.

(True story: I cleaned, searched, vacuumed, and scrubbed my house top to bottom, and first day of Passover this year, I discovered two ~~granola~~ bars of dust in my purse. Thanks to the above declaration, it's all good—I simply destroyed the evidence and removed it from the premises.)

The Seder

The holiday begins with lighting candles at sundown, as with every other Biblical holiday. A service is held at the synagogue, and then all families return to their homes to begin the Seder. It is a very strong tradition to have the Seder with lots of people, generally with one's extended family, and/or lots of guests. When an Israeli asks me what I'm doing for Seder this year and I say, "Just the five of us," I get a look that's halfway between pity and horror. Even Jews with very little connection to tradition and halakha tend to attend some kind of Seder. I guess the parallel would be how Christmas is celebrated so widely even by people who don't really consider themselves Christian. We like to have quiet, intimate Seders, so there's room for discussion, but things don't drag out too long, and especially when our kids got old enough to participate, we really want to keep their attention as long as possible. Back in the USA, we generally had our Seders with my dad's parents in New York and whatever aunts and uncles were around.

The word "Seder" means "order," referring to the ten steps of the ritual meal that must be carried out in order. The Haggadah, briefly mentioned in the letter about the Jewish holy books, guides us through these steps, which mostly involve reading the passages aloud and eating symbolic foods that help us commemorate those events. The symbolic foods are arranged at the center of the table on the Seder plate: parsley for *karpas*, salt water, horseradish, or romaine lettuce for *maror*, some brown, mortar-like mush called *charoset*, a shank bone, and an egg.

We also set three matzot on the table in a pile and covered by a cloth.

The table is set, the kids and guests are seated, and we begin:

Kadesh (Sanctification)

The leader of the Seder (usually the head of the household) recites the Kiddush over a cup of wine. This is the same kind of "declaration" of the sanctity of the day that we perform on Shabbat and other holidays. If the Seder falls on a Friday night, the Kiddush for Shabbat is recited as well. Then, we all drink our first cup of wine while reclining. This is symbolic of our freedom, as royalty used to eat while reclining. (Yes, I said "first" cup of wine. There are four. It's gonna be a long night.) Grape juice is okay for those of us who would rather remain sober...

Urchatz (Washing)

We wash our hands as though for bread, but without the blessing. We're not about to eat bread, but the custom is to wash our hands this way before eating a food that is dipped in liquid.

Karpas (Green Vegetable)

We eat a green vegetable, usually parsley or celery, dipped in salt water. The green vegetable symbolizes spring, and the salt water symbolizes the tears we shed under the oppression of slavery. The Polish tradition is to do this with potato, which is not a green vegetable, but good luck finding anything green in Poland at this time of year.

Yachatz (Splitting in Half)

The leader of the Seder takes the middle matzah from the pile and breaks it in half. The bigger half is hidden away as the *afikoman*, which will be eaten later.

Maggid (Retelling)

Maggid is the centerpiece of the Haggadah, the section that actually contains the retelling of the story of the Exodus. There's no way I'm going to cover all its contents here. For that, you'll have to actually read a Haggadah. You'll notice that it doesn't really follow the narrative the way you'd expect. To understand why... well, you'll just have to come to our Seder someday, and we can discuss it long into the night—as per the tradition!

So, by this point in the evening, if you've never been to a Seder before, you're going to be really confused. What's going on? Why are we eating these weird things? Why is this holiday so different from other holidays?

Well, that's how Maggid kicks off the story. The smallest child at the table recites the Four Questions: "*Why is this night different from all the other nights—that on all other nights, we eat chametz and matzah, but on this night, only matzah? That on all other nights, we eat all kinds of vegetables, but on this night, we eat bitter herbs? That on all other nights, we don't dip our food even once, but on this night, we dip it twice? That on all other nights, we eat sitting or reclining, but on this night, we all recline?*"

The idea of the Seder is to make the children curious so they will ask questions like these.

The answer to those questions comes right away: once, our ancestors were slaves in Egypt, and God saved us from their hands. The text then dwells a little on the concept of retelling the story and educating our children about the Exodus, and then goes on to describe the story of the Exodus and interpretations of the passages and events by various Sages. (Remember, the Haggadah is an extremely old text that was written around the time of the Talmud, so the passages reflect rabbinic discourse of that period.)

The most poignant part of the Seder, in my view, is the following passage, recited in the middle of Maggid: "*And it is [that promise] that has stood for our fathers and for us, for not only one has arisen against us to destroy us, but in every generation they arise against us to destroy us, but the Holy One, Blessed be He, saves us from their hand.*" This line, written so many centuries ago, has rung true at every single Seder since.

Rachtza (Washing)

We wash our hands again, this time actually for bread—that is, for...

Motzi Matzah

That first word refers to the blessing we make over bread, *hamotzi lechem min ha'aretz,* "... *who brings bread out of the ground.*" We make two blessings over the matzah—one for the enjoyment of food, and one for the mitzvah—and eat the prescribed amount of it while reclining.

Maror (Bitter Herbs)

These are eaten to represent the bitterness of slavery. We usually eat either romaine lettuce or horseradish or some mixture of both. We first dip the lettuce or horseradish into a brown mush called charoset, which represents the mortar used by the slaves to make the bricks. It is traditionally made with apples, wine, nuts, and/or dates, and is supposed to be sweet, so it sweetens the bitterness of the herb representing slavery.

Korekh (Sandwich)

Now we follow a tradition established by Hillel the Elder in the days of the Second Temple. Tradition has it that Hillel sandwiched all the symbolic foods of Passover—the matzah, the maror, the charoset, and the Passover sacrifice (a lamb)—and ate them together. Since we have no Temple, we cannot make the sacrifice, so we leave out the lamb. By the way, if you're still wondering about the shank bone and the egg on the plate—the bone represents the Passover sacrifice, and the egg represents the Chagiga (holiday) sacrifice.

Shulkhan Orekh (Setting the Table)

This is where we have the feast—everybody's favorite part! Traditional foods include *knaidlach*, or matzah balls, dumplings made of ground matzah, in chicken soup; the aforementioned gefilte fish, which are balls of ground fish, usually carp; and lamb, in commemoration of the sacrifice. (I happen to dislike lamb. So, beef or chicken it is. As for gefilte fish, usually I can take it or leave it, but I enjoy it as a special Passover thing.)

Tzafun (Hidden)

So remember the piece of matzah the leader of the Seder hid away way back before Maggid? Now is the time to find it: it's the afikoman (that word apparently comes from the ancient Greek for "dessert"). We're required to have a prescribed amount of it as the last thing we eat. But first, the kids have to find it. Another treasure hunt! This is a great way to keep them awake and engaged. Another tradition developed out of this is that the children then hold the afikoman "captive," thereby indefinitely delaying the end of the Seder, and bargaining to give it back in return for a gift or a treat.

Barekh (Bless)

Now we recite Grace after Meals, over a third cup of wine (the second was drunk at the end of Maggid), and then drink that cup and recite the blessing after drinking wine. The final cup of wine is poured.

Hallel (Praise)

Hallel is a special prayer recited on holidays, comprised of Psalms 113-118. The first part of Hallel is recited at the synagogue, and it is continued here, and then we go on to read additional psalms along the same general theme of God being awesome. The final cup of wine is now drunk. (And if it's really wine, so are we!)

Nirtzah (Acceptance)

The title of this final part of the evening refers to God accepting our completion of the Seder. This is when the Seder officially ends. (There are opinions that this is not a distinct section of the Seder, but that this and the previous are one section—Hallel Nirtzah.) We sing *l'shana haba'ah b'yirushalayim habnuya*—"next year in rebuilt Jerusalem"! Then there are a few more traditional Passover songs, which are generally fun and lively and get everybody's energy up for the final leg of the Seder. (Great for keeping the kids awake, too.)

The very last song of the Seder, at least in Ashkenazi tradition... you'd think it would be something profound, about freedom, or the purpose of the Jewish people, or maybe even about the holiday itself. But actually, it's a cumulative song in Aramaic about a little goat that Dad bought for two zuzim (units of money), which gets eaten by a cat, which gets bitten by a dog, which gets hit by a stick, which gets burned by a fire, which gets doused by water, which gets drunk by an ox, which gets slaughtered by a shochet (ritual slaughterer), who gets killed by the Angel of Death, who gets destroyed by the Holy One, Blessed Be He...

(And you betcha we sing it with sound effects!)

... I know. Why on earth do we end the Seder with this silly little ditty?

Obviously, as with everything in the Seder, because it has important symbolism. The idea of the song is that there is justice in the world, even if we don't see it at the time; that every action has a consequence, and that, as the Talmud says: *"There is justice and there is a Judge."*

Believe it or not, this silly animal song contains the deepest, most fundamental message of the Seder.

Why is it so important for us to remember that God freed us from slavery and brought us out of Egypt?

Because we must remember that there is justice, and there is a Judge, and even when the world seems unjust and terrible things are happening to good people, there is a reason for everything, and it's all for the ultimate good. Even when we're in the profoundest depths of despair, God's redemption can occur in the blink of an eye.

That is the message of the Seder, and that is why the tradition of the Seder has carried us through many other "Egypts" throughout history.

So... that's the Seder, in a nutshell. Outside of Israel, you get to do the whole thing all over again the following night. (I'm sure there are advantages to this, but to me, it just sounds exhausting, and I'm grateful to be here!)

A blessed and happy Passover!

Love,
Daniella

In the Empty Synagogues of Poland

Dear Josep,

Holocaust Remembrance Day is observed in Israel starting this evening, on the 27th of Nisan, which is the day the Warsaw Ghetto Uprising began. The date was also selected for its proximity to Memorial Day (for the fallen soldiers and terror victims) and Independence Day next week. We see all these events as part of the same story.

We observe this day with ceremonies, stories, lowered flags, and sad music on the radio, and one thing that is unique to Israel: a siren sounds throughout the country at 10 am, and everyone stops whatever they are doing, stands up, and observes two minutes of silence in memory of the victims of the Holocaust. The entire country comes to a literal halt.

As you can imagine, remembering and teaching about the Holocaust (the Shoah in Hebrew) is a big deal in the world's only Jewish country, and given that Israel was founded out of the ashes of the Holocaust and on the backs of its survivors, it's a major part of our national identity. Educating future generations about it is of utmost importance to us. To this end, many high schools arrange educational tours to the death camps in Poland.

In the Empty Synagogues of Poland

There's some controversy about those trips; about the moral integrity of funding Poland's "death camp tourism" industry, about whether those rowdy teenagers actually get anything meaningful out of the trip, and about whether the Holocaust should be something so deeply focused upon and ingrained into our national identity when we have 3,000 years of rich and diverse history to draw upon. After all, half of the country's Jewish population is comprised of non-Ashkenazim: Jews from North Africa, the Middle East, India, and Ethiopia. They have other important stories to tell, stories that are not told as thoroughly and as publicly as the stories of the Ashkenazim. Furthermore, some argue, is it really so healthy for such a major part of our national identity to be built upon a sense of victimhood?

Well, I traveled to Poland with my fellow 11th graders in March 2004, and it was one of the most powerful and meaningful experiences of my life, the kind of experience whose depth of its impact is completely impossible to convey to those who weren't there. But let me try.

We visited three camps: Auschwitz-Birkenau, Majdanek, and Treblinka, as well as the neighboring cities, Krakow and Warsaw, and a number of small towns where Jews once flourished, such as Lodz, home of the famous Hassidic sect, and the charming town of Tykocin... and the mass grave in the nearby Łopuchowo Forest where its entire Jewish community was murdered by the Nazis.

We had several guides, including an Israeli guide, a Polish guide, and a "witness": a man who survived the camps of Majdanek and Auschwitz and whose family was murdered at Treblinka. We're especially lucky to have been the last generation that could travel with a witness and hear his personal story as we stood at the very places where the events happened. Our witness, Avraham, was a remarkable man with a vibrant spirit and a great sense of humor, and his contribution to the trip was immeasurable. Our teachers accompanied us and ran discussion groups. Our principal had brought his guitar and he played along with our singing.

And we sang everywhere. We filled every empty synagogue with song and dance; we sang *Am Yisrael Chai*, "The Nation of Israel Lives," and brought life and music to all these places where our ancestors had been silenced.

In the gas chambers of Majdanek, we sat on the floor and sang about faith and yearning for redemption through our tears. It may sound strange to do anything but observe a reverent silence in such a place; but for us, raising our voices in song is our way of honoring those who died there, giving them a voice, calling out to God from the depths of our despair.

We walked, grandchildren of survivors, free citizens of a sovereign Jewish state, and sisters of the Jewish soldiers protecting it, down the infamous train tracks, into the forests, and through the remnants of the ghettos. We carried our Israeli flags with heartbroken pride; our unspoken message to those who died there that their deaths were not in vain. My friend, Menucha, whose grandmother survived Auschwitz, says: "I remember walking in Auschwitz with an Israeli flag on my back and thinking of how my grandmother had come in with nothing. I think it's one of the proudest moments of my life."

One evening in our hotel in Krakow, a woman came to speak to us and tell us how she and her family sheltered Jews during the Holocaust. After her talk, we got up, one by one, to thank her and hug and kiss her. That wordless exchange—the glowing warmth and gratitude, the firmness of her grip on my arms, the softness of her white cheeks against my lips—is burned forever into my memory.

There's no way to replace this kind of learning. As Menucha says, being there with a witness to share his story was like the difference between learning about the Shoah and being in Poland; the difference between knowing and feeling.

So did my trip, and the focus on the Shoah in my education, result in building my national identity on a sense of victimhood?

The answer is: absolutely not.

In the Empty Synagogues of Poland

It built my national identity on a deep sense of purpose and triumph. Triumph, because we are the answer to the Holocaust. Every Jewish baby born, every Israeli soldier sworn in, every mitzvah observed, every holiday celebrated, every song, every laugh, every smile... is another slap in the face of Hitler and all he stood for. Ultimately, we won; not with guns or bombs, but with our spirit, our faith, and our dedication to our identity and purpose.

"*The Eternal Nation is not afraid of a long journey,*" I sang with my friends in the empty synagogues of Poland. The Jewish people is here to stay. We have something invaluable to give the world. We have been oppressed, persecuted, and massacred for carrying that message for thousands of years. But we're still here, still carrying it. Learning the terrible extent of the sacrifice my brethren made to keep their identity and hold on to that message makes me all the more determined to do the same, and to pass it forward into what will hopefully be a brighter future for all of us.

Love,
Daniella

Israeli Emotional Roller Coaster Week

Dear Josep,

Today is Rosh Chodesh Iyar, the first day of the month of Iyar.

I recently saw a cartoon by Shay Charka that was printed in the Makor Rishon newspaper. It shows a steep roller coaster track with a man holding on for dear life, his kippah about to fly off his head. At the top of the hill he's coasting down is a yellow Jewish star with *Jude* written on it; at the bottom of the drop is a torch propped up with rifles; and then the track shifts into the blue stripes of the Israeli flag, with the blue Jewish star at the center, as it takes a sharp turn upwards.

This is a perfect visual representation of what the two weeks after Passover are like in Israel.

Toward the end of Passover, you start to notice some blue and white streamers popping up along the roads. Then, you start spotting teenagers at intersections, selling Israeli flags that fit onto your car window, usually around 15 NIS a pop. I can't tell you how many of these we've lost by opening the window while driving at high speed. A couple of years ago, they started selling these cute side view mirror covers that lack that disadvantage. Flags begin to appear on balconies and in windows.

Israeli Emotional Roller Coaster Week

At the top of the metaphorical roller coaster is Holocaust Remembrance Day. The importance of this to our national identity has already been described above in *In the Empty Synagogues of Poland*. A week later, we have Memorial Day, in honor of the fallen soldiers and terror victims. The very next day is Independence Day (Yom Ha'Atzma'ut), the 5th of Iyar, which is the day Ben-Gurion declared independence. Now, remember—Jewish days begin and end at sundown. So Memorial Day begins at sundown this Tuesday. At sundown on Wednesday, the whole country makes a sudden and very dramatic shift from solemn mourning to joyous celebration. This may seem kind of jarring, but to us it makes perfect sense. We cannot celebrate our independence without first expressing our gratitude to those who gave their lives for that freedom. Last week, we remembered the victims of the Holocaust, standing as a symbol of the culmination of all Jewish persecution and suffering over the centuries. Then, we acknowledge those who died for our country. Only then can we celebrate our national independence, the miraculous realization of a 2,000-year-old dream.

As a kid, I remember being struck by how Israelis seemed to connect less to Holocaust Remembrance Day than to Memorial Day. To me, the Holocaust was a tragedy so much more awful in every possible way. What I didn't quite understand at the time was that even grandchildren of Holocaust survivors tended to have much more up-close-and-personal experience with death in the context of wars and terrorism. There's not a single Israeli who doesn't have at least a casual connection with someone who was killed in a war or a terror attack. It's a small country. Serving in the army is mandatory after graduating high school. It's fairly impossible to avoid.

Memorial Day is observed similarly to Holocaust Remembrance Day. A one-minute siren sounds in the evening at 8 pm, and another, for two minutes, at 10am the following morning. Flags are lowered, ceremonies are held, graves are visited, and candles are lit.

As you may remember, I didn't serve in the army; I chose an alternative available to people who prefer not to serve for religious or moral reasons (usually religious women) known as national service (sherut leumi). You may recall that I worked in the northern office of OneFamily Fund, now called One-Family Together, an organization that provides emotional, legal and financial support for victims of terror. I could probably write an entire book about what that year was like for me, but one thing that it helped me understand was how very, very close these tragedies were to all of us.

This year, unfortunately, over seventy names will be added to the list. Most of them are soldiers who were killed during Operation Protective Edge this summer. Some of them are people who were killed in the vehicle and stabbing attacks while those were "popular" back in the fall. (Actually, another man was just killed in a vehicular incident, but it hasn't been confirmed that it was a terror attack.)

There are a few people I will be keeping in mind when the memorial siren sounds.

One is a young lady named Karen Yemima Mosquera. She was from Ecuador, the daughter of a family with what appear to be crypto-Jewish roots, and she came to Israel to study and make a formal conversion to Judaism. She had completed her conversion process just a few months earlier, and had just begun her life as a fully observant, formally recognized Jew. She was killed when a terrorist veered his car into a crowded train stop, in the same attack that killed a three-month-old baby. I didn't know her personally, but somehow—probably because of my connection with Spanish crypto-Judaism—her story touched me deeply.

Another is a woman from my community. Just last week I was looking at an old Google spreadsheet that listed the names and phone numbers of potential babysitters, and my stomach fell when I saw her name there.

And of course... three of those new names are the names that make every Israeli heave a deep sigh. The names we were posting on social media, chanting in rallies, hanging on signs, wearing on shirts... and then singing mournfully, spelling out using candles, and using to name new initiatives: Eyal, Gilad, and Naftali.

After these twenty-four hours of painful memories, on Wednesday night, we blow out the candles, raise our flags, and celebrate, with public ceremonies, parties, fireworks, and concerts. In the religious Zionist (*dati leumi*) communities, a special prayer is held after the usual evening prayers, singing various psalms and verses of praise, and Psalm 126 to the tune of HaTikva.[32] For us, Yom Ha'Atzma'ut is not only a national holiday, it is a religious holiday. We see the foundation of Israel as a miraculous historical event much like the events that we celebrate during Chanukah and Purim. Older Israelis, secular and religious alike, like to hold *shira b'tzibur*, "public singing," which is a sort of communal version of karaoke, where the music is played and the words displayed on the screen but everybody sings together.

As a teenager, I would walk to downtown Rechovot with my friends, where the main streets would be closed to traffic, and there were vendors selling candied apples and other treats, and various Israeli-flag-themed paraphernalia, usually including big blow-up plastic hammers with which kids bonk each other on the head. Don't even ask me how this became a Thing, but kids also run around spraying each other with "snow foam" and colored spray streamers. Well, I guess it's slightly better than Venetian scented eggs.[33]

---

[32] *HaTikva*, "The Hope," is the Israeli national anthem. Within the first twenty minutes of my very first conversation with Josep, he informed me that he knew all the words to this song, and took a deep breath as if to start singing, but thought better of it, seeing as we were standing in a little street corner print shop in Barcelona around a bunch of other young people who thought both of us were weird enough to begin with. It was at this point in our conversation that I started to wonder if maybe I was hallucinating.

[33] There used to be a custom to throw eggshells filled with perfume at a lady one wished to court during the carnival in Venice. Apparently this has been outlawed.

Anyway, during the day, it's become something of a tradition to have a picnic, usually a barbecue, probably because the weather tends to be just right for it and basically any excuse to eat a whole lot of meat sounds good to an Israeli. Many people dress in blue and white in honor of the holiday, and cakes, cupcakes, and cookies are decorated with Israeli flag toothpicks or blue and white frosting or sprinkles. Special prayers are held again for the morning services. Museums, tourist sites, and public parks are open and often admittance is free. The IDF also opens some of its lots to the public, where people can come look at the equipment they use up close. In general, Yom Ha'Atzma'ut is a day to honor and celebrate the soldiers who protect us, so it's also customary to give them gifts and have kids write them thank-you notes.

And then, we have a couple weeks' break until the next minor and somewhat obscure holiday on the calendar: Lag B'Omer.

Love,
Daniella

Israeli Emotional Roller Coaster Week

Counting Up: The Omer and Lag B'Omer

Dear Josep,

This part of the year is chock full of notable events on the Jewish calendar. The next one coming up is Lag B'Omer, which is pretty much the most obscure holiday we have. But before we get into that, let's back up a minute and talk about the Omer.

What is the Omer? Well, the word itself refers to a certain offering that was brought to the Temple at this time of year (*omer ha'tenufah*, "the sheaf of waving.") But it also lent its name to something we call "the counting of the Omer" (*sefirat ha'omer*).

Remember how we mentioned that the Exodus was basically the birthday of the nation of Israel? Sometimes it is also compared to the "betrothal" between God and the Israelites. The betrothal, or engagement, is an initial commitment that takes place before the eternal commitment of a marriage, right? So if the Exodus was the "betrothal," the giving of the Torah—the seal of the eternal bond between us and God—is the "wedding."

When a bride and groom are looking forward to their wedding, they often count the days left until the big day. That's exactly what counting the Omer is—only when we count the Omer, we count *up*, instead of *down*.

Counting Up

And you shall count from the day after the day of rest, from the day that you bring the omer ha'tenufa, *seven complete weeks. Until the day after the seventh week, you shall count fifty days.*
(Leviticus 23:15-16)

It just so happens that I got married on the 47th day of the Omer—the 3rd of Sivan, three days before Shavuot. So that year, that feeling of counting up in anticipation was very tangible for me!

The "day of rest" referred to in the above passage is the first day of Passover. So we begin the night after. Since this is a mitzvah, we make a blessing first, and then count the first day: "Today is one day of the Omer," "Today is two days of the Omer," etc. Note that the passage says to count both seven *weeks*, and fifty *days*; so we mention both when we count. For instance, today is day twenty-five, so last night the formula went as follows: "Today is **twenty and five days**, that are **three weeks and four days** of the Omer."

So why are we counting up instead of down?

Good question.

According to the Kabbalah, there are ten ways that God expresses Himself in the universe. These attributes or emanations are called *sefirot*. Does that word sound familiar...? They are, from highest to lowest: *keter/da'at* (crown/knowledge), *binah* (understanding), *chokhma* (wisdom), *chesed* (loving kindness), *gevurah* (might, discipline), *tiferet* (beauty, glory), *netzach* (eternity or mastery), *hod* (splendor), *yesod* (foundation), and *malkhut* (sovereignty). These sefirot are arranged in a certain order, from the lowest and most material, to the highest and most spiritual. The lower seven are the ones that are expressed in our world.

This is not the time or place to expound upon each one of these attributes, how they are expressed in the world and how we can recognize God through them. Kabbalah is a whole world unto itself and I don't know much about it.

Anyway, each day of the Omer is associated with a different combination of sefirot. The first week is chesed, loving kindness, so the first day is "the chesed within the chesed," the second day is "the gevurah (might/discipline) within the chesed," etc.

The point of this is that it's an opportunity to examine the way each of these attributes is expressed *through us*. So for instance, today is "the netzach within the netzach." Netzach can be interpreted as "eternity," or "mastery," or "endurance." So on this day, we can think about our endurance, our consistency, our fortitude, and try to improve these qualities within ourselves.

So let's return to the question: why are we counting *up?* Because the idea is that with each day that passes from Passover to Shavuot, from the Exodus to the Revelation at Sinai, we rise up a spiritual level. Today, we are on level twenty-five—halfway there! Tomorrow, we will be on level twenty-six. When we reach level fifty, we'll be ready to re-accept the Torah. Using the chart of the sefirot is one way that we can help ourselves ascend the spiritual ladder that is the Omer.

Now. All this is very exciting and you'd think that this would be a joyous time of year. Right?

Well...

Around the time of the destruction of the Second Temple, there was a rabbi called Rabbi Akiva. He is mentioned often in the Talmud as one of the greatest and most influential teachers of his time. He had thousands of students, and at one time, there was a terrible plague that killed off 24,000 of his students during the first thirty-three days of the Omer. The Gemara states that this plague was wrought upon the students "because they did not honor one another." For this reason, during the first thirty-three days of the Omer, it is customary to be in a sort of symbolic public state of mourning. We don't cut our hair, don't shave beards, don't buy new clothing and don't have weddings.

Now... one might ask, why all the fuss and bother over a bunch of students who died 2,000 years ago? Haven't there been worse disasters in our history that might be more deserving of public displays of mourning? Heck, if we commemorated every major disaster in our history, we'd be in mourning every single day of the year.

Well, it's a good question. And you know how we Jews sometimes like a good question better than we like a good answer...? The answer to this question is not so neat and easy to explain. People can take it in all kinds of different directions. One article I read went through the historical details of exactly what happened with the hypothesis that these students had the potential to reverse the destruction of the Temple and bring on the era of the Messiah, but that, because they didn't honor one another, they failed to do so and created an extremely unfortunate turning point in our history. This is the best explanation I have heard.

So what is Lag B'Omer then? "Lag" is simply the number thirty-three. Hebrew letters are also used as numerals, so thirty-three is ל"ג, which, sounded out, says "lag." The thirty-third day commemorates three things:

1) The end of the aforementioned plague;
2) The death of Rabbi Shimon Bar Yochai, to whom the Zohar (the book of the Kabbalah) is traditionally attributed, so it's a big day for Kabbalists;
3) The rebellion of Bar Kokhva against the Romans (after the destruction of the Second Temple) began that day. (The rebellion eventually failed, but... the same way we feel pride about the Warsaw Ghetto Uprising, which also eventually failed, we also feel pride about Bar Kokhva's uprising.) To communicate the beginning of the rebellion, Bar Kokhva's men lit bonfires to be seen by their colleagues...

And that is why Lag B'Omer is the most polluted day of the year in Israel.

It has become a custom to light bonfires in honor of Bar Kokhva that night. Now, Israelis love bonfires. It's a big part of traditional kibbutz culture, and fits right in with the general

Israeli love of being outside. (And didn't I mention that Jews have a thing for fire?)[34] So this custom is a big hit even among totally secular Israelis.

Lag B'Omer is next week, so all the kids are hard at work collecting bonfire wood, hoarding it, and guarding it ferociously from other kids. When I was an older kid and young teen, I enjoyed going to bonfires with my friends, roasting meat and marshmallows in the flames, and staying up late hanging around the fire.

But then I grew up, got sick of dealing with all the smoke, and became a curmudgeon along with my asthmatic husband, so this is the only night of the year we keep all our windows closed and the air conditioner on all night...

Love,
Daniella

---

[34] See: *A Nation of Pyromaniacs*.

Counting Up

Why Jerusalem Matters

Dear Josep,

The 28th of Iyar, 5727 (June 7th, 1967) was a historic day for the Jewish people. It was the day our eternal capital, Jerusalem, was reunited, and we regained access to our holiest site—the Temple Mount.

Yes, I said the Temple Mount. Because while the Western Wall is generally known as being the holiest site in the world for Jews, that isn't actually true. The Western Wall was just the retaining wall of the platform on which Herod's renovated Second Temple stood 2,000 years ago. What was so important to us was the Temple itself.

I keep mentioning this Temple, and it's been many years since I explained to you what it was.

So in honor of Jerusalem Day, which we will celebrate this coming Sunday, let me tell you the story of the Temple and of Jerusalem.

HaMishkan (The Tabernacle)

After we received the Torah at Mt. Sinai—an event on which I will elaborate soon, as Shavuot is right on the heels of Jerusalem Day—God commanded the Israelites to build something called the *Mishkan*, the Tabernacle. ("Mishkan" means "dwelling place.") It was a sort of portable structure that contained a courtyard and a tent (the Tent of Meeting).

The courtyard contained the Copper Altar, which was used for the ritual sacrifices that were made there regularly as part of our service of God, as well as the washstand (for ritually washing hands—that's where our tradition of washing before eating bread comes from!)

The Tent of Meeting contained two chambers. The outermost chamber was called the *Kodesh* and contained the Menorah, the Table with the twelve "showbread," and the Golden Altar (for incense).

The innermost chamber was called the Holy of Holies, and, as the name implies, it was the holiest place on Earth for us, wherever it was at the time. Only Moses and Aaron were permitted to enter, and only at designated times; and after their deaths, only the High Priest could enter, and only on Yom Kippur at a specific time during the service. What was so special about this place? It contained the Ark of the Covenant, the gold-plated box that carried the original Tablets of the Covenant that Moses received at Mt. Sinai, upon which the Ten Commandments were inscribed.

Beit HaMikdash (The Holy Temple)

We carried the Mishkan with us through the desert, and eventually, when we settled in the Land of Israel, the Mishkan was set up permanently, not in Jerusalem, but in Shilo. Shilo is a little town in Samaria, and recent excavations there are uncovering what may very well be the place where the Mishkan once stood. (This is one of Eitan's favorite places to take tourists. It's an amazing site.) Samuel the Prophet was conceived after his mother Hannah prayed at the Mishkan in Shilo, and he was raised there by the High Priest, Eli, until he became a prophet. (See the opening chapters of Samuel I.) Samuel was the prophet who crowned the first kings of Israel: Saul and David.

It was King David who first raised the idea of building a Temple, a permanent structure for the Mishkan. "*See now*," he said to Nathan the Prophet in Samuel II 7:2, "*I live in a house of cedar, and the Ark of the Lord dwells within curtains.*" God, however, did not want David to build His house, and the Sages say that this is because David fought many wars and "his hands were stained with blood." God wanted the Temple to be built in a time of peace. So He promised David that he would have a son who would continue his dynasty, and that son would build the Temple.

And that's what happened. King Solomon, son of David, built the First Temple in Jerusalem on the Temple Mount. Religious scholars place its construction at around 832 BCE.

Why a Temple?

Let's back up a second here. We're talking about the world's first monotheistic religion—the first religion to worship a single, omnipresent God who was not manifested in any physical object or person. So why would we center our worship of Him around a physical building, and the physical objects therein? Isn't that a little too much like the idol worship we were supposed to be obliterating?

When instructing Moses on the construction of the Mishkan, God said, "*They shall make for me a Temple, and I shall dwell within them.*" (Exodus 28:8) Notice that He didn't say, "dwell within **it**." The idea was not for God to manifest Himself in a physical object or place. He said "dwell within **them**"—the People of Israel. **The Mishkan was not for *Him*, it was for *us*.** It was meant to orient us toward Him and His service, so that awareness of Him would dwell within us. We never worshiped the building or its contents. They were tools that we used to worship God.

I heard a wonderful class by Rebbetzin Tzipora Heller about teaching one's kids about the Temple and its importance. She suggests giving an explanation like this: "You know how sometimes, when you get home from school, you can tell that Mommy's already home, even if you don't see her or hear her voice? Maybe you see her coat hanging in the hall, or you smell her perfume, or there's just something about the way the house is different when Mommy's home. That's like what it was with the *Shekhina*—God's presence—at the Temple. We can't see Him or hear His voice, and of course He is everywhere, all the time. But when we had the Temple, we could really feel His presence."

The Temple was the place where God and man embraced, where the limited physical reality of human existence touched the eternal. The very physical work that the service of the Temple involved—the sacrifices, the contributions, the incense, the rituals—was a way to tangibly connect with God. And that's why our entire religion, our entire service of God, originally centered around the Temple.

Why Jerusalem?

The first mention of Jerusalem in the Bible, according to our tradition, is in Genesis 22—Mt. Moriah, where Abraham brought his son Isaac to be sacrificed. It came under Israelite control in the time of King David, who captured it from the Jebusites. The name *Yerushalem* or *Yerushalayim* first appears in the book of Joshua. The source of the name is unclear. Our Sages teach that it is a combination of the name Abraham gave the site of the (aborted) sacrifice of Isaac, *[Hashem] Yira'eh* ("God will show Himself") and the town of Shalem. The root sh.l.m. (ש.ל.ם.) means "peace" or "whole."

King David made Jerusalem the capital of the tribe of Judah, and of the Kingdom of Israel. Aside from the mystical implications (Isaac's sacrifice and Abraham declaring that spot a place where God will show Himself), this was a highly practical choice. It was a defensible mountain on the border of Judah and Benjamin, close to the center of the kingdom, with the necessary water sources and a good climate for agriculture.

Letters to Josep

Jerusalem is also known as Zion, Ir HaKodesh ("the Holy City"—or in Arabic, *Al-Quds*) and the City of David, among others.

A Portable Judaism

Here's the thing, Josep. Judaism, as a religion, has undergone great changes in the thousands of years it has been around. And the biggest changes were a result of the destruction of the Temple, which forced us to shift from a service that centered on that physical space, to a "portable" service that we could carry with us throughout exile.

The significance of this shift, and the fact that it was able to happen at all, cannot be taken for granted. As I mentioned, when the Temple stood, our service of God looked very, very different from the way it looks now. Animal and produce sacrifices and contributions were made regularly and for varying reasons and purposes, some of which were burned on the (copper) altar and some of which were consumed by the priests (Cohanim) or the Levites. The three major holidays were characterized by a nationwide pilgrimage to Jerusalem. All men were required to make that pilgrimage at least three times a year. **This is what the "original Judaism" looked like.**

When the First Temple was destroyed, the leaders of the Jewish community had to figure out how to keep Judaism alive in Babylonia. It was then that the institution of the synagogue was first established. As I mentioned in the letter about the Jewish holy books, when we were granted permission to return to Jerusalem and rebuild the Temple, the leaders Ezra and Nehemiah established a number of practices to keep Jews connected to the Torah and to the Hebrew language. The Second Temple was built under their leadership. It was that Temple that was defiled by the Greeks and rededicated by the Maccabees. The building was later expanded by King Herod under the Romans. Jesus was born while it still stood, and it was destroyed by the Romans seventy years after his birth.

Why Jerusalem Matters

After the destruction of the Second Temple, Judaism encountered another huge crisis. The study and transmission of Jewish Law were forbidden under Roman law, and great teachers risked—and gave—their lives to continue teaching and passing on the tradition. The framework of halakha that we use today to apply the Law to current circumstances was solidified during this period. The Oral Law, which was originally not supposed to be written down, was nonetheless preserved in writing in what eventually became the Talmud. The global center of Jewish thought and development now shifted to Babylonia and the great schools of Sura and Pumbedita. Jews continued to live in the land of Israel wherever they were allowed until the modern era, but the ritual practice of Judaism had successfully adapted itself to exile.

Nonetheless, for 2,000 years, we have continued to mourn the destruction of the Temple and to yearn for Zion. We have begged God to return us to our homeland and "renew our days as in the old times." Our dream is to return to the original practice and closeness to God that we experienced when the Temples stood. For 2,000 years, at the close of every Passover Seder and Yom Kippur fast, we have proclaimed: "Next year in rebuilt Jerusalem!" This, for us, is the Messianic vision. Zionist Jews such as myself believe that the establishment of a sovereign Jewish state in Israel is *at chalta d'geula*—"the beginning of the redemption" in Aramaic; a step on the way to the Messianic Era. (Unfortunately, we still seem to have a long way to go.)

The month after Shavuot, we will enter a period of mourning for the Temple that has been practiced and preserved throughout the Jewish diaspora. The Ninth of Av, the day the Temples were destroyed, is still the saddest day of the Jewish year, and a major fast day second only to Yom Kippur. For two millennia, Jews prayed and cried at the remaining wall of the Temple, which became known as the Western Wall, or the Wailing Wall. In Israel, we simply call it the Kotel—"the Wall."

During the War of Independence in 1948, the Jordanians took control of the Temple Mount and the Old City, so when the State of Israel was finally established, our most treasured parts of Jerusalem were not part of it. But on that fateful day in June, 1967, an emotional cry was heard over the army radio: "The Temple Mount is in our hands! The Temple Mount is in our hands!" When the fighting died down, throngs of Jews flooded to the Western Wall to pray and give thanks to God for returning our precious holy site to our hands, the first time in 2,000 years that the Temple Mount was under Jewish sovereignty. To this day, we celebrate Jerusalem Day with a lively procession from the center of town to the Western Wall, where there is singing and dancing and great rejoicing.

But.

After the war, the Israeli government handed the keys to the Temple Mount over to the Waqf, the Muslim authority of the Al-Aqsa Mosque. The idea was to maintain freedom of worship on the holy site, which is a given in any democratic country, and Israel is no exception. Muslims and Christians alike are granted free and unrestricted access to any holy site under Israeli jurisdiction. Unfortunately, the Waqf does not share this philosophy. Jews and Christians are only allowed to visit the Temple Mount through prearranged agreement, with organized groups and under careful supervision. We're not allowed to pray on the Temple Mount, nor to bring any written material, lest it be some kind of religious text. Theoretically, these rules apply to any non-Muslim, but practically, Jews are singled out for severe treatment. Jews are kept in a small, closely accompanied groups, and are continuously heckled by Muslims shouting at them wherever they go on the Mount. Numerous Jews have been detained for the "crime" of standing silently with their lips moving. A rabbi was recently forcibly removed from the premises for responding, "*Hashem hu ha'Elokim*" ("The Lord is God") to a man who shouted, "*Allahu akbar*" ("God is great") at him.

The situation is completely absurd.

The Temple Mount is definitely not in our hands.

To me, it's so ironic that the holiest and most important site in Judaism is the only place in Israel where the basic human right to religious freedom does not apply to Jews (or to Christians). And it is absolutely infuriating to me that this is the status quo and that this issue is not even part of the discussion about the Israeli-Arab conflict. The unrest that erupted in Jerusalem this past fall was partly due to a rumor spread among the Muslims of some kind of Jewish plot to take over the Temple Mount. **We don't want to take over the Temple Mount. We just want to be able to visit and pray there freely.** The Cave of the Patriarchs in Hebron is holy to Jews and Muslims alike, and there is a perfectly acceptable arrangement there that allows people of both religions to pray and worship there without incident—despite the fact that Hebron is also a focus of great political controversy. It is beyond me why a similar arrangement at the Temple Mount would be so offensive and threatening to Muslims.

Isaiah prophesies that when the Messiah comes: "*Also those sons of other nations that join the Lord to serve Him, and to love the Name of the Lord, and to be his servants... I shall bring them to My holy mountain, and make them joyful in the House of My Prayer... **for My House shall be called a House of Prayer for All Peoples**.*" (Isaiah 56:6-7)

Amen, may it be His will.

Love,
Daniella

Shavuot:
On Covenants and Cheesecake

Dear Josep,

The Shavuot holiday coincides with a number of joyful events in my family. In 2008, Eitan and I got married three days before Shavuot. In 2009, I gave birth to my eldest son the morning before Shavuot. In 2012, I gave birth to my third son right on the day between our anniversary and his oldest brother's 3rd birthday! Understandably, the Omer "count-up" has special meaning for us every year.

So what is this holiday and what is its significance?

"Shavuot" literally means "weeks." The word *shavua* comes from the root sh.v.a., ש.ב.ע., which means "seven." But that same root also means "oath." Remember how I said that Passover is like the birthday of the Jewish people, and that Shavuot is like the wedding anniversary? The 6th of Sivan is the day God gave us the Torah at Mt. Sinai. In the fifty days between the Exodus and receiving the Torah, we went from being slaves to prophets—every one of us.

In Rabbi Judah the Levi's philosophical work *The Kuzari*, he puts forth an argument that is still used in theological debates when discussing the Divine origin of the Torah. He states that every other religion began through the revelation of a single human being—Islam had Mohammad, and Christianity had Paul. (Yes, Jesus before that, but Christianity as its own religion, as opposed to a Messianic sect of Judaism, basically began with Paul's revelation.) The thing about individual revelations is that they are impossible to verify. You can either believe that Mohammad or Paul was a true prophet and had a true revelation, or not. A skeptic could easily claim that they were making it up or were clinically insane, and it is very hard to prove or disprove one way or the other.

It gets a little harder to dismiss when you make the outrageous claim that an entire nation stood at Mt. Sinai and personally heard God speak. We're talking about around 3,000,000 people. It is extremely difficult to argue that 3,000,000 people went simultaneously insane, or just got together and decided to make the whole thing up and tell their children and their children's children that they personally heard God speak, and manage to pass that intact story down through every generation for 3,500 years.[35]

Now, this is obviously not a flawless argument—there is no such thing when it comes to theology—but it is a fairly strong one, and certainly differentiates Judaism from the rest of the world's religions. Only Jews would have the audacity to claim that our ancestors all stood at Mt. Sinai and heard God speak with their own ears.

According to Exodus 19-20, the nation gathered at the mountain on the 6th of Sivan, and God gave them the Ten Commandments. (This, by the way, is a fairly inaccurate translation of that phrase. We have 613 commandments, not just ten, and these ten aren't necessarily more important than the others. The Hebrew phrase *asaret hadeebrot* is more accurately translated as "the Ten Statements.") The Israelites were so overwhelmed by the Divine revelation that they told Moses to go up to the mountain and receive the rest of the Torah for them. He ascended Mt. Sinai and received the Tablets of the Covenant.

---

[35] You can find a detailed explanation of this philosophical approach in Rabbi Lawrence Kelemen's book *Permission to Believe* and his classes on the topic that can be found online, such as "A Rational Approach to the Divine Origin of the Torah."

So What's the Deal with this Torah Thing?

In my *Introduction to the World's Biggest Book Club*, I gave two definitions for the Torah, the first of which was: "the entire body of teachings and Jewish law, starting with the Bible and all the way down to the rabbinic literature being written at this very moment."

Now, one might ask oneself, aren't we talking about faith and a relationship with God? What about this dry, austere collection of legalistic rulings and restrictions is so important and inspiring to Jews that they were willing to sacrifice their comfort, safety, financial viability, and sometimes their lives for it, for 3,500 years?

Here's where our wedding allegory comes back. The Torah is like a wedding contract. If you take a look at any type of prenuptial agreement, you're most likely to encounter a bunch of boring legalese. Any kind of contract provides the framework, the boundaries through which a healthy, prosperous relationship can grow.

A good example of this is Shabbat. If you sat and read through those books I showed you about the laws of observing Shabbat, all you'd see is a whole bunch of things you're not allowed to do. How stifling and restrictive! But as you saw yourself, all the "thou shalt nots" are not what define Shabbat. Shabbat is so much more than a bunch of restrictions. It is a time outside of time, a space to disconnect from our role as "creators" and enjoy our role as "creations." We could not fully feel and enjoy this if we didn't have a way to clearly differentiate our existence on that day from that of every other day of the week. The laws of Shabbat provide the frame; we fill in the picture. This is, of course, also true about marriage.

So what is the Torah? **The Torah is our contract with God and our handbook to creating a just, moral, God-conscious society.** God made a covenant with us to use the framework of the Torah to create a better society and raise the spiritual level of humanity to a point where God will be able to reveal Himself to all. He wanted us to do this by serving as an example to the rest of the world, being a "light unto the nations," as it were. In return, He promised to give us the land of Israel—a land at the center of the world, where the paths of the leading civilizations at the time constantly crossed, meaning that they would all come into some kind of contact with us. He promised to bless us and protect us and provide for all our needs, as long as we kept our end of the deal.

That didn't exactly go as planned, but that's a story for the Three Weeks and Tisha B'Av.

Celebrating Shavuot

Shavuot is one of the Three Regalim—the Biblical holidays on which we were required to make a pilgrimage to the Temple in Jerusalem. Like the other Biblical holidays (Passover, Rosh Hashana, Yom Kippur, Succot, and Shmini Atzeret), it is observed similarly to Shabbat, with restrictions on "acts of creation"—with the one exception of certain actions required for making food. In Israel, Shavuot is one day long; outside of Israel, it is two days.

Other than that, there are no specific mitzvot associated with Shavuot. It's customary to express our gratitude and love for the Torah by staying up all night learning Torah. (Eitan likes to note that this custom only came into existence when coffee became widely available.) Many synagogues are specially decorated with flowers and colorful cloths to cover the Ark (where the Torah scrolls are kept) and the Torah scrolls.

According to tradition, King David's birthday and date of death were both on Shavuot. For this reason, we read the scroll of Ruth during services on Shavuot, which tells the story of David's great-grandmother, a Moabite convert to Judaism.

Another well-known custom of Shavuot is to eat dairy products. Tradition has it that this is because when the Israelites received the Torah, they were overwhelmed by all the laws regarding kosher meat, and decided to make life easier on themselves by just eating dairy until they were on top of the whole kosher meat thing.

Unlike in most areas concerning cuisine (in my opinion, anyway), my Ashkenazi ancestors did dairy pretty well. Classic Ashkenazi dishes include blintzes (like fried crepes), bagels (traditionally eaten with cream cheese and smoked salmon), and cheesecake; the latter has become the classic Shavuot dessert.

Shavuot falls on this coming Sunday, which means that we Israelis are in for a two-day Shabbat-Yom-Tov, and non-Israelis are in for a three-day extravaganza.

There will be cheesecake.

Lots of cheesecake.

So Shavuot doesn't exactly follow the formula of "They tried to kill us, we won, let's eat." But at least there's the "Let's eat" part!

Love,
Daniella

Shavuot

Starving for God: Jewish Fast Days

Dear Josep,
 The 17th of the Jewish month of Tamuz falls on this coming Shabbat. It marks the beginning of the period we call the Three Weeks, which culminate in the major fast of Tisha B'Av, the day the Temples were destroyed. But I'll get to that in a later post. The 17th is observed as a minor fast day. But this year the fast will be observed the following day—the 18th—because we're not allowed to fast on Shabbat. (Yom Kippur is the only exception to this rule.)
 Virtually every religion on Earth has some tradition of fasting. For Jews and Muslims, this means refraining from partaking in any kind of food or drink during the day. For Catholics, and other Christians who practice fasting, it's a lot more—shall we say—open to interpretation. At most, it means going without food, but not water. And it usually means reducing one's intake or refraining from certain types of foods, generally food that has been historically considered high-class or festive such as meat, dairy, eggs, and the like.
 Well, while I'm wasting away without food or water on a sweltering summer day while my kids run hyper circles around me and destroy the house, I'll think of you, dear Christians, and your self-imposed temporary veganism, and I will shed a

tear. (That's a whole drop of water that could have been in my cells. You should be deeply moved.)

Ahem. Now that I've got that out of my system:

Why Fast at All?

Why is it that so many religions have this tradition of restricting or refraining from eating or drinking? I think at its most basic, this is pretty simple to explain: eating and drinking are some of our very basic animal needs, but free will was given to humans by God, and fasting is using that free will to distance ourselves from our animal nature, therefore bringing us closer to our spirituality and to God.

Now, if you've been *really* paying attention all these years I've been gabbing at you about Judaism, you'll be asking, "Wait. Aren't you always saying that Judaism is all about sanctifying the mundane and channeling our basic human needs for a higher, holier spiritual purpose—in direct opposition to other religious concepts of distancing ourselves from the mundane?" You're absolutely right. In Judaism, the way we normally relate to the basic animal needs of eating and drinking, is to sanctify them—be that by using them to celebrate the Sabbath, a holiday, a mitzvah (such as a wedding or circumcision ceremony), etc., or by simply reciting a blessing over the food.

Why do we fast, then?

So the thing is, in Judaism, fasting is less about spiritual uplifting, and more about expressing grief, sadness, and regret. You know how when you're really stressed out or depressed, you can't bring yourself to eat anything? That's what fasting means to us. Fasting is what we do as an expression of communal grieving, or to express the regret that's essential to the process of repentance. That isn't to say that we don't believe in fasting as a means to spiritually cleanse ourselves and/or bring ourselves closer to God the way it is done in other religions; it's more of an "and" than an "either/or."

The Jewish Fast Days

As I have mentioned before, there are two major fasts on the Jewish calendar. They are **Yom Kippur**, and **Tisha B'Av**. Both of these fast days are entire letters in and of themselves, so I'm not going to get into too much detail here; I'll focus on the aspect of fasting.

Yom Kippur is unique among the Jewish fasts in that it's the **only** Biblically prescribed fast, and also the only fast day that is also a holiday. On Yom Kippur, God commands us to refrain from five things—eating and drinking, sexual relations, washing, wearing leather shoes, and anointing ourselves with oil. The Torah says specifically that the purpose of this abstinence is to "cause ourselves to suffer." If we do this on Yom Kippur, He promises, and sincerely repent for our sins, He will "wipe the slate clean." (See *Days of Awe* for more on Yom Kippur.)

The other fasts in the Jewish calendar are all rabbinic.

- **Tisha B'Av**, the other major fast day, is the day both Temples were destroyed, and has generally been a particularly, shall we say, unlucky day for the Jewish people. (See *Between the Dire Straits* for more on Tisha B'Av.)
- **The Fast of Gedaliah**, a minor fast which falls the day after Rosh Hashana, mourns the assassination of the leader of Judah after the destruction of the first Temple, killed by another Jew due to political disputes. If not for this murder, there may have been a hope of maintaining a significant and continuous Jewish presence in the land of Israel even under Babylonian occupation. The murder signified the nail in the coffin of the first Jewish commonwealth in the Holy Land.
- **The 10th of Tevet**, which falls soon after Chanukah, was the beginning of the siege of Jerusalem by Nebuchadnezzar, which culminated in the destruction of

the First Temple a few hundred years before the Common Era. (The exact date of the destruction is under dispute.)
- **The Fast of Esther**, which takes place the day before Purim, commemorates the fast that Queen Esther of Persia observed as she planned to risk her life by visiting King Achashverosh to ask him to spare the Jews.
- **The 17th of Tamuz** commemorates the Roman breach of the walls of Jerusalem that led to the destruction of the Second Temple.

Major vs. Minor Fasts

There are several differences between major and minor fasts:

1) **Duration**: Major fasts begin at sundown and end at nightfall the following day, meaning they last twenty-five hours. Minor fasts begin at daybreak and end at nightfall the same day, so they usually last somewhere between fourteen and eighteen hours (longer in the summer, obviously).
2) **Restrictions**: On minor fasts, we are only prohibited from eating and drinking. On major fasts, we are also prohibited from the other four "afflictions" of Yom Kippur—sexual relations, washing, wearing leather shoes (considered to be a luxury back in the day), and anointing ourselves with oils or perfume. On Tisha B'Av, since it's a day of mourning, we also have some restrictions to do with mourning, such as sitting on low stools and avoiding listening to music.
3) **Strictness**: Yom Kippur is the strictest of them all. In fact, the punishment the Torah lists for eating on Yom Kippur is even more severe than that of breaking Shabbat. As a rule, every Jew above the age of mitzvot (twelve for a girl, thirteen for a boy) is required to fast.

But obviously, if fasting would put one's life in danger, one may not fast. People who must eat and/or drink, by doctor's orders, if possible, do so in small amounts at fixed intervals (less than "a cheekful"—around 30ml—of liquid and a matchbox-full of food every four to nine minutes); this allows them to technically "fast" according to the guidelines of the Sages. If they can't do this, they eat and drink normally. All Jews (barring children and those with a doctor's order not to fast) must fast on Tisha B'Av, too; but if one has a medical reason not to fast or to break the fast, he eats and/or drinks normally, since it is a rabbinic fast and therefore less severe. Pregnant and nursing women, as a general rule, are required to fast on Yom Kippur and Tisha B'Av, but a woman should **always** speak to a doctor and a rabbi she trusts before fasting to get specific guidelines for when and how to eat and/or drink if she starts to feel unwell. On minor fasts, on the other hand, anyone who is ill is automatically exempt (many rabbis include pregnant and lactating women as well) and if one starts to feel ill or weak enough that one must lie down during the fast, one is allowed to break it.

Isn't Fasting Torture?

This is such a First World Problem. Thank God that in our day and age people have no idea what it might be like to go an entire day without eating or drinking.

Everybody experiences fasting differently; some people are hardly affected at all, and some people are totally incapacitated by it. Most people feel kind of weak and shaky by afternoon, maybe a little dizzy; some people get headaches. Many people feel a kind of adrenaline rush toward the end of the fast, where suddenly they feel more energetic and kind of lightheaded; the mood during Ne'ilah, the last prayer of Yom Kippur, often reflects this.

For most people, me included, it's not exactly fun, but it's not all that bad, either.

Breaking the Fast

In contrast to Ramadan, there's no special meal on which Jews break their fasts. On Yom Kippur, the festive meal is actually eaten *before* the fast. On Tisha B'Av we also have a symbolic "last meal" before the fast, sitting on the floor with some bread and salt (symbolizing the poverty of our ancestors under siege) and a hard-boiled egg with ashes on it, to symbolize our hope for the rebuilding of the Temple out of the ashes.

So when the fast ends, we simply eat and drink normally. In Israel, there are always articles going around before Yom Kippur about what to eat before the fast (lots of "light" protein, like fish or chicken, and "slow carbs" like whole grains that take longer to digest) and after the fast. After going a full day without eating and drinking, it's recommended (from a medical standpoint) to start with some juice or other sweet drink to rehydrate and get your blood sugar back up, accompanied by a light snack like cake or crackers; then, after a little while, to have a bigger meal. Many synagogues offer some drinks and cakes to congregants after the services on Yom Kippur.

Okay, so, what's so very terrible about the destruction of the Temple, that we designate four fasts, including a major one, to mourn for it?

Stay tuned, and you shall have the answer.

Love,
Daniella

Between the Dire Straits

Dear Josep,

So, the Three Weeks.

I mentioned before that the 17th of Tamuz marks the beginning of a period of symbolic mourning for the destruction of the Temples in Jerusalem. Practically speaking, what this means is that we observe the same customs of symbolic mourning that we do during the first thirty-three days of the Omer: we don't attend live concerts (and have varying customs on what kind of music we listen to), don't buy new clothes, and don't get haircuts (and men don't shave their beards). In Hebrew, the period of the Three Weeks is called *Bein HaMetzarim*. This is could be cleverly translated into English as, "Between the Dire Straits." (Since you are not a native English speaker, I want to make sure you understand this: "Meitzar" is both a "strait," as in a channel connecting two bodies of water, and a flowery Biblical word for trouble or distress. "Dire straits" is an English expression that means "very serious trouble.") The Sages teach that this is a period during which "the Prosecutor[36] speaks against us," meaning that God judges us more harshly. So we try to kind of "lay low" during this period,

---

[36] Meaning Satan. See: *The Vagueries of the Jewish Afterlife*.

avoiding important business interactions or other endeavors that require Divine assistance.

From the first day of the month of Av (or if you're Sephardi—which, um, I guess you are!—from the Saturday night before Tisha B'Av) the symbolic mourning intensifies. Ashkenazim call this period the Nine Days. Sephardim call it *hashavua shechal bo*, "the Week on Which It Falls." We no longer bathe for pleasure or wash our clothes (unless it's necessary for hygienic purposes), and we don't eat meat or drink wine. (I guess you Catholics might call that fasting.) We also do not build houses or move into new homes during this period.

"Tisha B'Av" means "the Ninth of Av," and it is the saddest day in the Jewish year. On this day, the First Temple was destroyed by the Babylonians, and then, by Divine poetry (or bizarre coincidence, for those who believe in such things) the Second Temple was destroyed by the Romans on the same date several hundred years later.

It so happens that a number of other great calamities befell the Jews on this day on the Hebrew calendar, and during this period in general. The last Jew left the shores of Spain on Tisha B'Av in 1492. A number of disasters connected to failed attempts to restore Jewish sovereignty over Judea after the destruction of the Temple also happened on Tisha B'Av. So, too, with a number of critical events during the Holocaust. Heck, just last year, I was rudely awakened on the morning of Tisha B'Av by an air raid siren... Like I said. Not a good time for the Jews.

So as I elaborated in my letter about Jewish fasts, Tisha B'Av is a major fast day, meaning that we refrain from eating, drinking, washing for pleasure, wearing leather shoes, anointing ourselves with oil, and sexual relations, from sundown to nightfall the next day. We also sit on low stools, like mourners sitting shiva,[37] for the first part of Tisha B'Av (until midday, at which point the Temple had already been destroyed); nor do

---

[37] See: *Processing Grief: Jewish Mourning Customs*.

we greet each other, because we're not allowed to greet mourners, and we're all mourning on this day. On the evening of Tisha B'Av, after the usual evening prayer service, the book of Eikha (Lamentations) is read in the synagogue while everybody sits on the floor. It was written by Jeremiah the Prophet and describes the desolation in Jerusalem after its conquest by Nebuchadnezzar. Then a series of *kinnot* (poetic lamentations) are read.

At midday on Tisha B'Av, we begin a gradual process of emerging from mourning. We may sit on normal chairs from midday. After the fast ends at nightfall, we continue to observe the mourning customs of the Nine Days, until midday on the following day, the 10th of Av. The reason for this is that the Temple was still burning until midday on the 10th. Then we fully emerge from mourning.

So. Obviously, this destruction-of-the-Temple business was seriously bad news for the Jews. One might ask: why? Why don't we fast to commemorate other great disasters in Jewish history, like the Holocaust, or the Cossack massacres, or the Crusades, or the expulsion from Spain, or... sheesh, take your pick, we'd be fasting every day of the year!

First of all, before you can understand why the *destruction* of the Temple was such a big deal, you have to understand why the *Temple* was such a big deal. I elaborate on this in *Why Jerusalem Matters*, so if you haven't read that letter yet, now is the time to do that.

In any case, in that letter, I wrote: "The Temple was the place where God and man embraced, where the limited physical reality of human existence touched the eternal. The very physical work that the service of the Temple involved—the sacrifices, the contributions, the incense, the rituals—was a way to tangibly connect with God. And that is why our entire religion, our entire service of God, originally centered around the Temple."

When God gave us the Torah, He had a vision for us. He would be our God, and we would be His people. The Holy Temple would serve as a meeting place between humanity and the Divine, not only for the Jewish people, but for the world in general. We were to serve as a model nation, showing the world what a society could look like if it follows God's word. We were to be a "light unto the nations" to spread morality and knowledge of God throughout the world. God promised us that if we kept His commandments and stayed loyal to Him, He would bless us and protect us, and make us a "nation of priests." A majority of the book of Deuteronomy is a speech that Moses gives the nation of Israel in which he goes over the commandments again, along with God's promise. But, God said that if we failed to keep the commandments, and strayed to worship other gods, He would curse us, and send us scattered from the land.

Basically, God presented us with an Ultimate Plan for the Redemption of the Universe. The plan was: we inhabit the land and set up a model kingdom right in the heart of the world, on the crossroads between Asia, Africa and Europe, where most world civilizations would have the chance to come in contact with us, and thus influence them to give up idolatry and immorality and embrace God and Godliness.

Unfortunately, we failed to create this model society. We succumbed to the temptations to be like other nations, to serve other gods, including our own "evil inclinations," and eventually God had to fulfill His promise: He destroyed our kingdom and our Temple. We lost our direct connection to Him. According to Judaism, there has been no prophecy since the destruction of the First Temple. The last of our prophets was Malakhi.

The rest... I'm going to step my current self aside and give my twenty-year-old self the stage. This is an excerpt from a ridiculously long letter I wrote to you eight years ago on Tisha B'Av, July 24th, 2007:

So you see... it's not really the destruction of a building I'm mourning as I sit here close to the floor with my face unwashed and my stomach empty. It's the destruction of a certain kind of relationship. When we were in this land with our Temple, we were so close to God. We were living as a "light unto the nations," a kingdom to shine as an example to the nations of the world and let them see how a fair and just society can look like. But we blew it.

My eyes fill with tears as I write this. We blew it. We failed. We broke the covenant. And God could not let us live here, together, any longer. He had to disperse us among the nations, where we would be hated and persecuted for 2,000 years, where we would be massacred and expelled and tortured and ridiculed throughout the centuries. Don't you see?

The destruction of the Temple is the root of all Jewish suffering.

If we hadn't ruined it, if we hadn't been so stupid, none of that would have been necessary to teach our lessons to the world! We wouldn't have needed to suffer so much to spread our ideas! All of it, all those coincidences on Tisha B'Av, and all those massacres during the Crusades, and the Spanish Inquisition, and the expulsions from everywhere, and the pogroms, and the Holocaust—all of it was part of the Divine Plan B, implemented after we messed up Plan A.

So what now? It seems that God is knocking on our door again, by some miracle giving us back the Promised Land and Jerusalem... but again, the world is poised against us. Will we mess it up again? Or will we somehow succeed in taking this chance to reestablish that role we've been missing for 2,000 years?

Right now, I feel the urgency of this question as our government and our society slide downhill. God doesn't need a Jewish people in its land with leaders who lie and cheat and sexually abuse.[38] He doesn't need a Jewish people in its land selfish and divided. I do believe—with all my heart—that bringing us back to Israel was the beginning of the process of redemption... but I'm so afraid of the shaky ground on which we stand. What if He has to destroy this process and go through it all over again?

---

[38] A few weeks before I wrote the excerpted letter in 2007, then-president of Israel Moshe Katsav resigned from his presidency after being accused of rape and sexual harassment. He was eventually found guilty, and he's currently serving a maximum sentence of forty-nine years in prison.

So we fast and we pray and we hope that we are strong enough, that we are ready to be what He wanted us to be. The whole purpose of the Jewish faith is to hone us into a model society, one that is loving and helpful to all others, that supports those who need support, and trusts in the One God and believes only in Him. On Tisha B'Av we long to become that society... without more suffering. Without more slaughter and bloodshed and hatred. We mourn the days that we had the chance to be that way, and we pray for a second chance in the days to come.

And that, my dear friend, is the meaning of Tisha B'Av.

May we all merit to see the redemption of humanity soon—whatever you believe that may mean.

Much love,
Daniella

Jewish Concepts

Different Kinds of Jews, Part I: Jewish Cultural Identity and the Diversity Therein

THIS LETTER is the first in a two-part "revamp" of a letter originally written to Josep in May, 2014, and a follow-up question he asked. I posted the reworked version on the blog a year later. Even though I expanded it enough to make it two entries, this topic is still so vast that I felt the need to make a big disclaimer: these categorizations are *extremely* general. I stuck to the ones that are most prominent and well-known.

Dear Josep,

You asked: "It has always struck me how Judaism is both a religion and a cultural group. How can you differentiate those? And how do you live those discrepancies?"

As an observant Jew, I don't differentiate them. They are completely interlocked.

Judaism as a 'Spiritual Citizenship'

Let me put it to you as an allegory. I would use Catalonia as an example but your weird political situation makes things messy.[39] Let's say you were born in Italy to Italian parents. So

---

[39] See *A Little Catalan Context*.

Different Kinds of Jews, Part I

for you, being an Italian means two things: 1) That you are part of the Italian nation/ethnic group, and 2) You are a resident of Italy. As an ethnic Italian, you are Italian no matter where you were born or where you choose to live. That's simply your DNA, and the culture of your parents. As a citizen of Italy, however, you enjoy certain rights and responsibilities, just by right of the fact that you were born there. So in this context, you can either be a "good" Italian citizen, who abides by the laws of his country, or a "bad" Italian citizen, who doesn't follow the laws of his country. Still, no matter what you do, you will always be Italian, whether you're a good citizen or not.

Now, I am not an ethnic Italian and I never will be. But say I decided that I wanted to become an Italian citizen... I can't simply declare myself Italian because I identify with the Italian cause, am a fan of Michelangelo and Vivaldi, and enjoy pizza. I would either have to have been born there, or I would have to undergo a process of absorption and live up to certain criteria—living there for a certain number of years, etc., and, of course, observe the laws of the place, before I would be accepted as a citizen by the Italian government and start to enjoy my rights.

So... being a Jew first and foremost means that you were born into the Jewish nation. That you are a descendant of Israel (Jacob). You *do* know why we're called Jews, right? The original Kingdom of Israel was divided into twelve tribes. After the rule of King Solomon, the kingdom split into two kingdoms: Judah (which included the tribes of Judah and Benjamin) and Israel (which included everybody else). The kingdom of Israel was destroyed by the Babylonians before the fall of the kingdom of Judah, and the ten tribes therein were believed lost to history. Today's Jews are all believed to be descendants of the inhabitants of the Kingdom of Judah. That is where the term "Jew" comes from—"*Yehudi*" meaning "from the tribe of *Yehuda*."

God didn't select us as a group with a common faith, but as a people with a common DNA. He gave the Torah to us as a sort of national contract, kind of like a constitution. We accepted it upon ourselves as a nation, and therefore we, as a nation, are obligated to keep it. **So you can think of the faith aspect of Judaism as a "spiritual citizenship" that is unique to the Jewish cultural group.** Being born into the Jewish nation automatically grants you the rights and responsibilities of that citizenship. Whether you choose to uphold those responsibilities does not change your ethnic status. A person born to a Jewish mother will always remain a Jew in my eyes no matter what faith he professes. But, as a Jew, I believe he has certain obligations that he's not upholding if he does not keep halakha. A person who was not born to a Jewish mother, however, does not have any obligation to keep the Torah, as he was not born into the "spiritual kingdom" of Judaism, and is, therefore, not bound by its constitution.

Having said that Judaism is a cultural identity, the fact that we have been scattered among the nations for so long means that there is great ethnic diversity within the unified ethnicity of Judaism. We call these subgroups *edot*.

Ethnic Subgroups Within Judaism

The main differences between the different ethnic subgroups, in terms of Jewish practice, are prayer liturgies and varying customs in how to perform the mitzvot (commandments). But we're all Jews: we all observe the same holidays and keep kosher, and for the most part, our lifestyles and beliefs are very similar. One reason Jews were historically so successful in business is that we maintained ties with our brethren throughout the world; we had more in common with each other than with the surrounding population. Some edot have holidays or traditions that are specific to them, like the Moroccan Maimuna and the Ethiopian Sigd, but the major holidays are the same. Israel can be a kind of melting pot of all these different cultures, and you'll find a lot of Jews marrying into other ethnic subgroups and creating interesting hodgepodges of these traditions and customs. As you may have noticed about me, I find

Different Kinds of Jews, Part I

other cultures fascinating and love to learn about the different kinds of Jews there are and how they do things differently. Anyway, here are the general ethnic categories:

Ashkenazi

Ashkenaz is the Hebrew word for what is now known as the general area of Germany/Austria. However, the term Ashkenazi refers to all Jews of Eastern European descent, including German/Austrian, Russian, Polish, Lithuanian, Latvian, etc. An overwhelming majority of Jews today are Ashkenazi—somewhere between 70%-80%.

Anyway, as you know, both Eitan and I are Ashkenazi Jews. My ancestors came from Ukraine, Poland, and Russia. Eitan's also came from those general areas, as well as Austria. Most American Jews are Ashkenazi, whereas about 45% of Israeli Jews are Ashkenazi.

Sephardi

Sepharad, is the Hebrew word for a certain peninsula on the far Western side of the Mediterranean. Something tells me you've heard of it.

You can find Iberia referred to this way in the last few books of the Jewish Bible, so I believe the term predates even the term Hispania. In modern Hebrew, it refers to modern Spain.

In general, people tend to refer to Jews as being either Ashkenazi or Sephardi, and this is not quite accurate, as you'll see in a moment. The reason North African, Middle Eastern, and Eastern Jews tend to be referred to as Sephardi is because, after the expulsion, the Spanish Jews who were forced to move to those places completely dominated the culture. So the next category—Mizrachi—overlaps with Sephardi in some places. Sephardi Jews—at least in the pre-Holocaust days—could be found in Italy, Holland, Greece, Turkey, and the Balkans as well as North Africa.

217

I should mention here that **Roman Jews** in Italy are sort of a category of their own in terms of customs and liturgy. But they are a pretty small minority.

Mizrachi

Mizrach means "east," and this is a general term used in Israel to refer to Jews of North African, Middle Eastern, or Eastern descent. This includes Moroccan, Algerian, Tunisian, Libyan, Egyptian, and native Israeli Jews (a.k.a. ones who lived in Israel before the establishment of the State and the "ingathering of the exiles") though, as I mentioned, many of these are also considered Sephardim. Other Jews who fall under the category of Mizrachi might be from India, Yemen, Iraq, Iran, Kurdistan, Bukhara, etc. Each one of these groups has distinct characteristics... and, of course, cuisine.

The reason that Sephardim and Mizrachim make up a majority of Israeli Jews, even though Ashkenazim are such an overwhelming majority is what you probably know from spending time in the countries of their origins: these places are very hostile to Jews these days. Many Mizrachim were forcibly expelled from their countries of origin when Israel was founded. Talk about a refugee problem. Some of them, like the Yemenites and the Iraqis, had to be rescued by the IDF.

I want to specifically mention **Bnei Menashe**, a group from India that claims to be descended from the tribe of Menashe (one of the ten tribes that vanished after the first exile). Since that connection has not been proven, they are not automatically considered Jewish by Orthodox standards, so many of them underwent an official conversion to Judaism and moved to Israel. There is a significant community of them in Kiryat Arba, the settlement right next to Hebron.

Ethiopian (Beta Israel)

The story of the Ethiopian Jews is a really amazing one. It is believed that the community first moved to Ethiopia during the time of King Solomon, and they were eventually cut off from the rest of the Jewish world, but they maintained many Jewish practices, including reading the Torah, keeping kashrut, and observing the Sabbath. They referred to themselves as Beta Israel, the house of Israel. There's speculation that they're descended from another of the lost ten tribes—the tribe of Dan. But because they were cut off from all the Talmudic and rabbinical discourse among Jews in other parts of the world, they did not observe many of the rabbinical laws that became part of Jewish tradition later. (For instance, they did not celebrate Purim or Chanukah.) They were officially recognized by the Israeli Rabbinate as Jews a few decades ago, and many of them were airlifted to Israel. They did have to undergo a conversion process to counter any doubts that remained (because there was some controversy about it in the Rabbinate) but most Ethiopian Jews in Israel today are considered completely Jewish.

Chinese/Kaifeng Jews

Yes, believe it or not, there is a small Jewish community in China that dates back hundreds and hundreds of years, which grew when Jews fled Europe during the wars. I have never met anyone from this community, but apparently they exist…

So as you can see, there is great ethnic diversity within the global Jewish community. And if anyone wants to argue that we are racist for not allowing intermarriage, that person will have to contend with the fact that a white Jew has much less of an issue marrying an Ethiopian, Yemenite, or Indian Jew than a white non-Jew. But I know you know the intermarriage thing isn't about race or any sense of superiority, but about preserving Jewish continuity—as we discussed in the past. Not to say that racism isn't a problem among Jews—just like it is among everybody else. Here in Israel, it's much more accepted than in the USA to stigmatize and make jokes about ethnic stereotypes. Ethiopians tend to deal with the worst of it. (There have been a number of big protests recently about racism against Ethiopian Israelis, and I hope that the dialogue on the topic that was created as a result will help improve the situation.) But Jews do tend to identify with people who have experienced similar struggles, and many Jews were involved in the Civil Rights movement in the USA during the 60s for this reason.

That concludes Part I. Next week, God willing, we'll tackle religious denominations and Hassidism.

Love,
Daniella

Different Kinds of Jews, Part I

Different Kinds of Jews, Part II: 2,000 Years of Arguing

THIS IS THE SECOND of a two-part "revamp" of a letter I originally wrote to Josep in May 2014. As with Part I, I must begin with a disclaimer: I'm a modern Orthodox American-Israeli Jew, and this letter (and the entire book, for that matter) reflects that perspective. So if you ask a differently affiliated Jew to define his or her community or other groups or subgroups, you may get different answers.

As before, there are many groups that will not be mentioned because this is a vast topic that could (and does) fill several books, and I'm sticking to the ones that are most prominent and well-known.

Dear Josep,

In Part I we addressed Jewish cultural identity and the subcultures within Judaism. But more well-known than the division between Ashkenazim, Sephardim, etc. is the division between Reform, Conservative, Orthodox and other denominations of Judaism. In this entry, we'll discuss how these movements came to be and how they differ from one another. We will also discuss Hassidism and its influence on Jewish practice and thought.

Religious Denominations/Levels of Religiosity

So this is where I get myself in trouble.

The first thing to understand about the idea of "level of religiosity" is that it's a fairly modern phenomenon. Up until the 19th century, there was no need to define a "religious" Jew because everyone was religious, and someone who abandoned the traditional practices of Judaism pretty much abandoned the faith and the community altogether. It was only at the time of the "enlightenment" in the 1800s, when Reform Judaism came about, that the concept of a "secular Jew" came into existence.

That said, throughout history, there were disputes between Jews on how to properly observe the Torah. (All together now: "Two Jews, three opinions...") At the time of Jesus, for example, Judaism was split into two major sects: the **Pharisees** and the **Sadducees**, who each had different ideas about how to observe the Torah. Mainstream Orthodox Judaism is basically descended from the tradition of the Pharisees. There is speculation that the **Karaites**, a movement that emerged around the 8th century, are the ideological descendants of the Sadducees. Karaite Judaism rejects rabbinic Judaism and the idea of the Oral Torah altogether, and believes that the written Torah must be observed literally. (Of course, the reason we *have* an Oral Torah is to interpret the many vague and difficult concepts in the Torah, so the Karaites developed their own tradition on how to interpret it.) There's still a small community of Karaite Jews, most of them in Israel.

Another thing that's important to understand is that the most well-known "denominations" today—Reform and Conservative—are mostly American. Reform Judaism began in Germany, but its center shifted to the USA as the Jewish population in the US grew and the one in Europe shrank due to emigration and the Holocaust. In Israel, the breakdown is a lot fuzzier, because as a general rule, Sephardim and Mizrachim tend to be less stuck on self-definition, and more traditional. I'll get to the Israeli definitions of religious level soon.

Orthodox Judaism

This is a general term for mainstream traditional Judaism: Jews who observe Jewish law as interpreted by the mainstream rabbinic authorities throughout history. The term "Orthodox" was borrowed from Christianity by the Reform movement, and I don't particularly like to use it to describe myself. I prefer to describe myself as an "observant Jew," meaning, I observe the commandments. But many people don't know what this means, so when speaking to people who aren't familiar with that term I usually use "Orthodox."

Within this category, you'll find the *charedim*, the "ultra-Orthodox," as well as "modern Orthodox." In Israel, "modern Orthodox" is mostly interchangeable with "Zionist religious" (or "national religious"—*dati leumi*), because charedim tend to be non-Zionist. Eitan and I consider ourselves dati leumi (see below under *Religiosity in Israel*).

Reform Judaism

Reform Judaism came about in the 19th century, when science became the new religion of Western society. Reformers saw the Torah and the observance of traditional Jewish law as outdated and superstitious. Basically, Reform Jews don't see the Torah as being binding in any way, and many of them don't believe that the Torah was given by God. If you ask a Reform Jew what he or she thinks the Torah is, you might get a wide variety of answers, but most would probably agree that it is a collection of wisdom (man-made, and perhaps "Divinely inspired") that they feel has value—only some of which is still applicable today. Many Reform Jews take ideas from the Torah (and the body of rabbinic teachings that they mostly reject) and apply them to modern Western values. A favorite is *tikkun olam*—"fixing the world"—which is actually a fairly vague, mystical concept from the Kabbalah, but is often applied to mean that man has responsibility to improve the world and make it a better place through social and environmental activism.

Different Kinds of Jews, Part II

Conservative Judaism

Conservative Judaism was a sort of counter-reaction to the Reform movement. Some Jews agreed with the Reform movement that Judaism needed some updating for the modern world, but did not want to reject the teachings of the Torah. So the Conservative movement started as sort of a middle ground between Orthodox and Reform. Conservative Jews do, for the most part, believe that the Torah is of Divine origin, but they believe that the Law is much more flexible than the Orthodox do—in that they don't see the precedents of previous generations as being nearly as binding as the Orthodox see them. They believe halakha is meant to be adapted as much as possible to modern times and reinterpreted to suit progressive sensibilities. So they tend to be more egalitarian and liberal than the Orthodox—mixed seating in synagogue, female rabbis, gay marriage, etc.—using their interpretation of halakha to find ways to permit things that Orthodox Judaism prohibits, for the sake of adapting to Western values. Practically speaking, however, in many Conservative congregations, the members of the community are not strict about observing the Conservative version of halakha, and there can be a huge gap between the level of observance of the rabbis and that of the congregants. In a sense, Conservative Judaism has become a sort of umbrella movement to include Jews who are anywhere on the spectrum between Orthodox and Reform.

Now... you being a secular liberal who has no solid opinion on the source of the Torah or its historical accuracy, I'm sure the above two movements make a lot more sense to you than the Orthodox approach. So you may be asking yourself, "Daniella is a reasonably intelligent, rational, open-minded person; why wouldn't she be on board, at least with the Conservative movement?"

So here's my personal take on "adapting halakha for modern times." I believe there's a reason God set up the halakhic system as we have observed it for thousands of years. While I identify with many "progressive" Western values, man-made

225

values shift and change over time, sometimes for better and sometimes for worse. I think the Torah is the expression of a value system that is eternal and Divine, and I believe that the Orthodox halakhic system is the most authentic way to interpret it in the way God wished. To me, adapting halakha to better suit Western values feels like taking a ring of the finest silver and coating it in stainless steel. It's taking a Divine value system and stuffing it into a fickle, man-made frame. I think serving God should be about adapting *yourself* to His system, not adapting His system to yourself. As I have mentioned many times, this isn't always easy, and the system is not perfect. Modern Orthodox Jews often struggle to reconcile our strong belief in the Torah and our identification with Western values when they seem at odds with each other. So I understand how others might feel differently about it. We live in confusing times, and God does not reveal Himself and His will the way He used to; we're meant to choose our path, and, growing up with so many different voices that sound reasonable and good, it's hard to know which path is the right one. I believe the Orthodox halakhic system is the closest to God's true will, so that's the one I try to follow.

There are other, smaller American denominations, but I'm not going to get into those as I don't know much about them. The above are the three major ones.

Religiosity in Israel

While Reform and Conservative communities do exist in Israel, for the most part they're extremely small and isolated, mostly of American or European immigrants. In most of Israeli society, it's a spectrum of observance, more than a set of strictly defined groups, but it basically breaks down like this. Secular Jews (*chiloni* in Hebrew) don't keep the commandments like kosher or Shabbat. The majority of Israelis are traditional Jews (*masorti* in Hebrew), who keep some of the customs and traditions, but not all. For instance, in a traditional Jewish family, they might make Kiddush over wine and

Different Kinds of Jews, Part II

light Shabbat candles, but then go watch TV. Or they might eat strictly kosher, but not keep Shabbat. It's really a continuum. Religious Jews (*dati* in Hebrew) are observant Jews who keep all the commandments, and those generally divide into modern Zionist (dati leumi), ultra-Orthodox Zionist (charedi leumi), and ultra-Orthodox non-Zionist (charedi). (Yes, there is such a thing as a non-Zionist Jew living in Israel. And their attitude to the state is a serious political issue.) Datiim leumiim are also sometimes called *kippah sruga* ("crocheted kippah") because they're the ones who wear colorful crocheted kippot, as opposed to the charedim who wear black velvet and/or black hats. (When you SMSed me to ask what color kippah to buy, I figured it was too complicated to explain the intricacies of these differences, and it didn't really matter anyway. I wasn't surprised to see that you inadvertently chose to identify with the religious stream Eitan and I belong to.)

Charedim keep a much stricter version of halakha than datiim leumiim, at least outwardly (modesty of dress, level of strictness about kashrut, separation between men and women in public, level of interaction with the secular world, etc.). Women are generally treated with respect, but there's a very strong focus on modesty and traditional gender roles, sometimes to an extreme that leads to marginalization and other unpleasant social issues. American charedim tend to be more open and progressive than Israeli charedim.

It's very easy to differentiate between datiim and charedim by the way they dress. Dati men wear kipot, may or may not have a beard and/or *payot* (sidecurls), may dress in regular casual clothes (T-shirts and shorts) or may dress more like Eitan—button down shirts and long pants. The women dress more or less like me: no restrictions on color, shirts with sleeves (the more religious you are, the longer the sleeve), skirts past the knee, and married women usually cover their hair to some degree, usually with a scarf or hat.

Charedi men wear black suits all the time, and the women wear only dark or pale colors, clothes that are non-form-fitting, stockings, and closed-toed shoes so the only skin you can see is their hands, face, and neck. Single women keep their hair tied back, and married women completely cover their hair, usually with a wig, but sometimes with a scarf or hat.

Now, as a Christian, you may note with curiosity that none of this categorization corresponds to *belief*. Whether someone believes in God or not does not actually define him religiously in Israeli culture. **Judaism is about what you *do*.** So you might find a completely secular Jew who believes in God and may even believe that the Torah is Divine, but just doesn't feel it's relevant to him. Or you may find a traditional Jew who doesn't really believe in God but thinks that the Jewish traditions are an important connection to his heritage and past.

Spiritual Approach (Hassidim vs. Lithuanians)

Another group you may have heard of is the Hassidim.

So what is Hassidism? It was a sort of Jewish renewal movement founded in the 17th century by a rabbi called the Baal Shem Tov. Up until that point, Judaism had become a kind of elitist society in which learned scholars were seen as being far more important than the common folk in terms of service of God. The approach was generally very dry, rationalist, and intellectual. The Baal Shem Tov sought to bring feeling and heartfelt service into the practice of Judaism. He also sought to teach that even the lowliest of peasants was just as important in God's eyes as the great scholars. This seems totally basic now, but back then, it was pretty revolutionary. There were a number of other ideas spread by Hassidism, one of which was the concept of the *tzaddik*, the "righteous person," who was a conduit to the Divine. Hassidim believed that by being close physically and spiritually to a tzaddik, they would be closer to God, too.

So as you can probably tell by now, parts of the Hassidic approach filtered down into most of Jewish practice today. But back then it was seen as a frivolous, anti-rationalist, and maybe even dangerous movement, and there was a strong counter-

Different Kinds of Jews, Part II

movement—the *Mitnagdim* (which literally means "the opposers"), led by the Gaon of Vilna (hence the term "Lithuanians.") He was a rationalist and felt that the Hassidim had their heads in the clouds and were not taking Jewish law seriously enough. This was a major, bitter schism within European Judaism that lasted pretty much all the way up until the Holocaust.

Nowadays, practically speaking, you can hardly tell Hassidim and Lithuanians apart. Hassidic sects tend to be ultra-Orthodox/charedi and dress in the same black and white garb. There are some distinct features of their traditional dress, such as the streimel, a round fur hat that some Hassidim wear on Shabbat and holidays. They do have a lot more singing and dancing than non-Hassidic charedi sects, and tend to be more involved in mysticism and Kabbalah. Non-Hassidim are more rationalist in their approach.

I mention all this because there are two particular Hassidic sects that are particularly relevant—the first because you're very likely to hear about them, and the second because I have a special connection to their philosophies and I'm likely to mention them in the future. Incidentally, both of them have a common feature: their rebbe—great rabbinic leader—is dead. (In every other Hassidic sect, there is a live rebbe who serves as the tzaddik and passes his status down through his sons and/or followers.)

The first sect is **Chabad** (spelled *Jabad* in Spain). They're also known as Lubavitch, the Yiddish name for the Russian village Lyubavichi, where the sect originated. These are the Hassidim you're most likely to meet because they're very involved in Jewish outreach and set up "houses" in all these random places all over the world where they offer all kinds of services to Jews who visit and live there. They tend to be very open and accepting in these contexts, and many people begin their journey of becoming religious through them. (As I just mentioned, Barcelona has a Chabad house, too. I was in touch with them before I came.) Their rebbe, Rabbi Menachem Mendel Schneerson (... "sch" is the Yiddish/German sound pronounced "sh"... sheesh, will the pronunciation confusion never end!) was a truly great man, and many of them believed that he was the Messiah. Some *Chabadnikim* still do believe this, which feels suspiciously Christian to the rest of us... but we love them anyway because they do great things!

The other Hassidic sect I want to mention is **Breslov**. Their rebbe, Rabbi Nachman of Breslov, lived in Ukraine in the 18th century and taught some really profound insights about despair, happiness, and developing a close and personal relationship with God. He is most famous for the following statements: "*All of the world is a very narrow bridge, and the main thing is not to make yourself afraid,*" and, "*If you believe that it's possible to destroy, believe that it is possible to repair.*" His followers practice a sort of meditation called *hitbodedut*, which simply involves talking to God like a friend, telling Him about all your troubles, asking Him for whatever you want, even the tiniest things. I really connected with this idea of a personal relationship as a teenager, and though I feel I have become more distant in recent years, I yearn to return to the simplicity of being in constant dialogue with the Creator this way.

Anyway, Breslov also attracts many *ba'alei teshuva* (people who start out secular and become religious) because of its deep and heartfelt philosophy. If you're ever in Israel and see a big white van decorated with all kinds of stickers and equipped with a megaphone stop at a red light, and a bunch of guys with long sidecurls, and big white knit kippot pile out, and start dancing in the street and on top of the van... don't call the police, that's just Breslovers trying to make people happy! Cultivating joy is a large component of their practice.

And thus we conclude Part II!

Love,
Daniella

Different Kinds of Jews, Part II

Happily Ever After: The Jewish Messiah

Dear Josep,

So as we rise from the floor this Tisha B'Av afternoon and begin to ease ourselves out of deep mourning for the Temple,[40] I thought it would be an appropriate time to look to the future, and write about what it is that we're praying for and hoping for when we talk about rebuilding the Temple.

Let's start from the beginning: what does "messiah" mean? It comes from the Hebrew word משיח, *mashiach*, which means "anointed." Back in the days of the Bible, you didn't crown a king, you anointed him with oil. King Saul, the first King of Israel, was anointed this way, as was King David. So the Messiah will be a king—a human king—from the line of King David, who will reestablish the Kingdom of Israel in the Holy Land.

The same prophets who predicted the destruction of the Temple (Jeremiah, Ezekiel, and Isaiah were the big three, but there were more) also foretold the coming of the Messiah. They described him as an individual with great wisdom and sensitivity, who will bring universal peace and justice. They described him rebuilding the Temple—one that will stand for-

---

[40] See *Between the Dire Straits*.

ever, and not be destroyed. They described the Messiah ushering in a new era, where all of humankind will know God and be aware of Him, and recognize the Jews as His chosen people. The Messiah will facilitate an "ingathering of the exiles"; Jews from all over the world will return to our homeland to establish the renewed Kingdom of Israel. We will stop being the hated and persecuted minority we still are today, and will reestablish our role as a nation of priests, who will be teachers and spiritual leaders for the rest of humanity. And people from all over the world will come to see the Temple—"a house of prayer for all nations"—and serve God there. Some scholars believe that the redemption will come about through miraculous means; others, including Maimonides, believe that it will happen in accordance with the laws of nature. Humanity will be on a completely different spiritual level, and the near tangible presence of God will again be felt at the Temple, where the human and the Divine will embrace. Prophecy—which, according to Jewish belief, stopped existing after the destruction of the first Temple—will return, with the Messiah being the first new prophet. And the world will be a place of harmony, peace, and love.

Now, reading this description, it's fairly clear why Jews did not accept Jesus as the Messiah. Simple: none of this happened. Not in his lifetime, and not in the 2,000 years since. He did not fulfill any of these prophecies. Now, Christian scholars would obviously disagree with me; they would interpret the same texts differently, and say that all this will come true when Jesus returns in a "second coming." But none of the prophets mentioned anything about the Messiah dying and then disappearing for a few millennia before coming back and fulfilling the prophecies. And *then* y'all started with the Trinity business.... and the thing about him dying for our sins... and that stuff is totally off the map of Jewish beliefs, so... yeah. The Jewish Messiah is not supposed to be Divine. He's supposed to be a human king and a prophet, just like David and Saul.

And there's no connection between him and atonement. That all goes down on Yom Kippur.[41]

Anyway. I think it's also fairly obvious from the above description why religious Zionists (such as myself) believe that the establishment of the State of Israel is a step along the way to the fulfillment of those prophecies. We have seen an "ingathering of the exiles"; we have seen the reestablishment of Jewish sovereignty in the Land of Israel for the first time in 2,000 years; we have seen the miraculous reunification of the city of Jerusalem; we have seen the land turn from a desolate wasteland into a thriving, fertile land flowing with milk and honey. We have even seen the Hebrew language, once a stagnant, archaic language reserved mostly for Jewish scholarship (not unlike today's Latin) turn into a living, breathing vernacular. These phenomena are baffling to historians, philosophers, and anthropologists. Nothing like this has *ever happened before*. It shouldn't have happened. It's impossible. And yet, it happened.

Still, going from the return of the Jews to their ancestral land—a phenomenon described as "spooky" by Nobel Prize laureate and physicist Leon Lederman—to a vision of all humanity living in peace and harmony and uniting around a single idea and belief in God is... quite a stretch.

Personally, I think of the Messianic Era as the culmination of everything we, as humans, strive for... and toward which we have already been advancing at breakneck pace, even though it may not feel like it. Because of how "plugged in" we are and how fast news spreads, violence, bloodshed, and turmoil seem worse than ever before, but the fact is that they aren't. There is actually *much* less violence in the world today than there was 100, certainly 200 years ago. Though the Middle East is falling to pieces and some crazy stuff is going down, it's a mere blip in the general trend, which is of a sharp decline in violence and oppression. We're so horrified by beheading and drowning videos, not because that type of cruelty is unprecedented, but

---

[41] See: *Days of Awe*.

because it has become so uncommon that we're not used to it. Think about it. Executions—beheadings, hangings, etc.—were a popular form of public entertainment less than 200 years ago. And that's without getting into the kinds of horrific things people used to do to each other in the Middle Ages and in the Roman Empire.

So, while we're very, very far from the "beating our swords into plowshares" thing, I don't think it's completely crazy to believe that sometime in the future, humanity will refine and improve itself to a point where the Messianic visions will no longer be visions, but reality. I believe that that's why we are here. That God wants us to bring the world to that point through free choice and free will. And I believe that it's possible... and that we're on our way there.

I know it's a pretty starry-eyed thing to be saying these days, especially from over here under the shadow of Daesh and a soon-might-be-nuclear Iran. You know me... to my sorrow, I'm not the world's most positive person, and sometimes (often) I despair, too. But if a nation could emerge from under the shadow of the Holocaust and turn this hunk of desert into a vibrant oasis of democracy and innovation after dreaming of Jerusalem for 2,000 years... who knows, Josep, who knows.

Love,
Daniella

A Nation of Pyromaniacs

Dear Josep,

So as you have probably noticed by now, Jews have a thing for candles. I think the photo I sent you on Friday demonstrates this pretty well: four *chanukiyot* (one for each family member above the age of three) all set up for the fourth night of Chanukah, with the Shabbat candles in the middle. Five for me, and one each for the kids over age three. Twenty-seven candles altogether, and we were only halfway through Chanukah! (And also some dirty dishes. We don't talk about those.)

Well, the truth is that most religions have a bit of a thing for candles. Fire is very ethereal, sort of on the borderline between material and spiritual, so it makes sense for it to be a spiritual symbol. In Judaism, the flame symbolizes the soul, because, just like the soul, it always rises upwards no matter which way you turn it.

In this letter, I will talk about the different kinds of candles we light in Jewish tradition and describe how and when they are lit.

But first, let's make an important distinction:

Menorah vs. Chanukiya

In English, both of these words generally refer to the nine-branched candelabras that are lit during the Chanukah holiday. But in Hebrew, those are only called chanukiyot. The menorah, on the other hand, is the solid gold, seven-branched candelabra that was one of the holy vessels in the Temple—the one the famed small jar of oil kept alight for eight days during the miracle of Chanukah. It is also the original symbol of Judaism, long before the six-pointed star became associated with Jews. Its central lamp remained lit at all times, and today, in many synagogues, you will find an "eternal lamp," a *ner tamid*, in commemoration of that lamp. (Nowadays, it's electric. Fire hazards, and all.)

The Chanukiya

So I assume you remember the story of Chanukah. The chanukiya has nine branches—one for each night of Chanukah, plus a "helper" candle, the *shammash*, which we use to light the others. We add one candle for every night, and light the newest candle first, moving left to right. The Ashkenazi custom is for each family member to have his or her own chanukiya. In Sephardi tradition, one person lights for the whole household.

You may have noticed that two of our chanukiyot have little glass cups filled with oil, and two of them have wax candles. Both are perfectly acceptable, but olive oil is halakhically preferred, for reasons I assume you can imagine.

The Shabbat Candles

Lighting Shabbat candles is one of the most well-known and faithfully kept Jewish traditions. Jews have gone to great lengths to light these candles—as in the classic image of the Converso lighting Shabbat candles in the basement or a closet.

Strangely enough, in terms of hierarchy in Jewish law, they're actually not among the most important commandments—not by a long shot. Though keeping Shabbat is a Biblical commandment of utmost importance, lighting the candles is not. It was instituted by the rabbis, and the reason given is *shlom bayit*—peace in one's home (the halakhic concept referring to harmony at home, particularly between husband and wife). What do candles have to do with familial harmony? Well... it's kind of hard to hold a nice family meal in the dark!

Yup. The Shabbat candles were instituted to prevent people from bumping into each other in the dark. How's that for anticlimactic.

On a higher level, of course, they have become a symbol of harmony in the home and an inseparable part of the ceremony of bringing in Shabbat.

Traditionally, two candles are lit, corresponding to the two slightly different versions of the Fourth Commandment in the Torah. (That's, uh, the Third Commandment for you. Catholics and Jews count differently.) The Bible gives two separate accounts of the Ten Commandments, almost identical, but not quite. In Exodus 20:8, it says: *"Remember the Sabbath day to keep it holy..."* and in Deuteronomy 5:12 it says, *"Keep the Sabbath day holy..."* The word for "remember" (*zakhor*) and for "keep" (*shamor*) are believed in Jewish tradition to have been said simultaneously, "within one word" at Mount Sinai. The candles correspond to zakhor and shamor.

So why do I have seven Sabbath candles?

It is a Hassidic custom to light an extra candle for every child in the household, symbolizing the light each child brings into our lives. My mother adopted this custom when she began lighting Sabbath candles, so I continue her custom. I have three children, so that makes five. The other two are for my older two kids to light themselves. Both men and women are obligated to have Shabbat candles lit, but in most households the woman performs this commandment for the family. Nonetheless, we educate our sons as well as our daughters to light the candles. My older sons are above the "age of education," age three,[42] so they both light candles.

And, you know, we try to begin cultivating ~~Jewish pyromania~~ fire safety habits as early as possible.

(You'll notice, though, that Shabbat candlesticks traditionally come in sets of two. Now that you know that the menorah is only lit on Chanukah, you'll just have to come back here and get yourself a pair of Shabbat candlesticks as well. You know, to light in the closet, in the tradition of your ancestors!)

The Havdalah Candle

So you thought we only light candles to mark the *beginning* of the Sabbath, did you? Nope! We light one at the end of the Sabbath too—but it has to be a special candle with multiple wicks. We usually use a special decorative, braided candle for this purpose.

Havdalah, meaning "differentiation," is the ceremony of closing the Sabbath and beginning the new week. The Havdalah candle symbolizes our return to work. While a single flame symbolizes the soul, fire is an expression of industry, of man's mastery over nature. After handing the world back over to God for one day—which is the essence of Shabbat—we are stepping back up to the plate in our mission to join Him in creating and perfecting the world.

The Memorial Candle

There is one more candle built into Jewish tradition, and that's the memorial candle. These are the long-burning candles we light to commemorate the dead. Traditionally, we light a candle that will burn for twenty-four hours starting at sun-

---

[42] See: *Links in the Chain: On Educating Children*.

down on the anniversary of a family member's death. In Yiddish we call it a *yahrtzeit* candle, yahrtzeit meaning "anniversary." In Hebrew, it's a *ner neshama*, a "soul candle." Their use has extended to commemorating the dead in other contexts. If you ever visit the death camps in Poland and Germany, you'll find lots of these candles at various monuments. And during public mourning vigils, like those held for the three teens this summer, lighting candles is how we express our sense of loss.

Happy Chanukah, and Bon Nadal to you and yours!
Daniella

P.S. I hate to say this, my friend, but "*Bon Nadal*" just doesn't have the ring to it that "Merry Christmas" does. I would say that even "*Feliz Navidad*" sounds better, but then you might hit me over the head with your Caga-tió.[43]

---

[43] The Catalan Christmas log. See *A Little Catalan Context*.

A Nation of Pyromaniacs

Teshuva:
As Long as the Candle Burns

THIS IS A COMPILATION of two e-mails I sent to Josep in 2014 about *teshuva*, or repentance.

Dear Josep,

You asked: "I may have asked this before, but I'm very interested to know more about how Judaism relates to guilt—being a "good"/observant/practicing Jew—and forgiveness."

As a religion, Judaism is just a lot less focused on guilt, forgiveness, and whether we are sinners or not, than Christianity. There are many possible explanations for this. My theory is that it's because Christians are mostly concerned with "saving their souls," which effectively means going to Heaven and avoiding Hell. Judaism is very different in this respect. Our primary concern is our conduct in this world and how to fulfill God's will while we are here. (See: *The Vagueries of the Jewish Afterlife*.) So, while we all consider ourselves sinners in some sense just because the Torah is basically impossible to keep 100% correctly, we don't dwell on it most of the time and it's just not an important feature of our day-to-day practice of Judaism. There is, however, one particular time during the year that we set aside for introspection and repentance, or teshuva.

Teshuva

And it's rather appropriate that you asked this question now, as that period is coming right up on the Jewish calendar. It begins in two weeks, with the month of Elul, building up to the High Holidays. (See *Days of Awe*.)

The following passage is part of a larger section toward the end of Deuteronomy, discussing the "blessing and the curse" that God gave the nation of Israel. It is considered the Biblical source for the commandment of teshuva:

> *For you shall return to the Lord, your God, with all your heart, and all your soul. For this commandment which I command you this day, is not concealed from you, nor is it far away...*
> *Rather, [this] thing is very close to you; it is in your mouth and in your heart, for you to do it.*
> Deuteronomy 30:10-14

The concept of teshuva is based on two fundamental principles in Jewish thought.

The first is that no matter how low a person sinks, no matter how horrible his actions, he is always capable of redeeming himself and changing for the better.

A story goes that Rabbi Israel Salanter, a famous rabbi who focused on the study of moral conduct and ethics, was walking down a dark street one night, and saw a faint light flickering in a window. He approached the window and saw a shoemaker repairing an old shoe by the light of a dying candle. Rabbi Salanter said, "Look how late it is! Your candle is almost extinguished. Why are you still working?" The shoemaker said, "As long as the candle burns, it is possible to mend." Rabbi Salanter was struck by the deep allegorical wisdom in those words. In Judaism, the flame is a symbol of the soul.

(This principle is, by the way, in sharp contrast to Christian thought, which argues that man is inherently sinful and is constantly pulled toward sin. According to Christian thought, the only way to redeem oneself from one's inherent sinfulness is to accept Jesus as having died to atone for it. In a sense, Christians also believe that "as long as the candle burns, it is possible to mend," but the Christian idea of "mending" is fundamentally different from ours.)

The second principle is that God is infinitely merciful and anxiously awaits our repentance. This is true in Christian thought as well. In the liturgy for Yom Kippur, there is a line that reads, "*Until the day of [man's] death, [God] will wait for him, and if he repents—[God] will immediately receive him.*" The image we have is of a God who is waiting for you with outstretched arms and great anticipation. He is like a father whose child has done something wrong, who is waiting anxiously for the child to say he's sorry, so He can embrace him, forgive him, and end the child's suffering from the distance between them.

The word "teshuva" comes from the root ש.ו.ב., sh.u.v., which means "to return." There's something very important to learn from this. It's not just about returning to God. It's about returning to yourself, to your "source." We are all created with a Divine soul, and underneath all the layers, we are totally pure and good. Teshuva cleanses us from those layers.

In another sense, however, teshuva changes us fundamentally. One might ask, I have done something so terrible, and my act was real and tangible. How can it simply be erased, as if it were no longer there? The answer, from the Jewish perspective, is that maybe the consequences of the sin still exist, but the person who committed that sin no longer exists. You are not him anymore, and when faced with the same temptation, you would turn away and not do what he did. Maimonides (who wrote a very important work on the practical aspects of teshuva) actually recommends symbolically changing one's name as part of the process to demonstrate that you're no longer the same person as the one who committed the sin. Bringing this together with the idea I mentioned in the previous paragraph, you are a different person—one who is closer to your source, to what you could be, to the potential of your Divine soul.

According to Maimonides, there are four steps to the process of teshuva.

Regret ("In Your Heart")

Notice that the word for this is "regret," not "guilt." The word in Hebrew for guilt is אשמה, *ashma*, which comes from the root א.ש.ם., a.sh.m., meaning "to blame." Guilt is self-blame. It is a natural emotion to occur when we've done something wrong, but it can lead us further down the spiral of self-destruction and negativity. Shame and guilt are the sense that there is something inherently wrong with you. The Hebrew word for regret is חרטה, *charata*, from the root ח.ר.ט., ch.r.t., which means "to chisel," "to smooth," "to engrave," "to refine," —to make a permanent and enduring change to something. **Regret is the recognition that you are inherently good, and you have failed to live up to your potential**, that what you did is not an expression of who you really are and who you really could be.

This is crucial, because obviously, if you don't genuinely understand what you have done wrong, you can't really change. And if you don't genuinely recognize your own potential to be someone who would never commit that sin, there's also no way to move forward.

Cessation

This part is fairly obvious. To repent for a sin, you have to stop committing it.

Confession and Asking Forgiveness ("In Your Mouth")

Both Christianity and modern psychology also recognize that thinking and feeling are not enough. We cannot truly be free of something that torments us until we have given it a name and spoken that name out loud.

There's no special formula for this in Judaism, and it doesn't matter where you are when you do it. All you have to do is speak to Him aloud, asking forgiveness, and explicitly naming what you did, in your own words. Unlike Christianity, this process is straightforward and does not involve a spiritual leader as intermediary. It's just you and Him.

Asking forgiveness from the person against whom you sinned is also a crucial part of the healing process—for both of you. Again, this has to be totally sincere. Whether that person is able or willing to accept your apology doesn't have a bearing on your process of teshuva; what's important is that you express your regret verbally to the person you hurt.

Resolution Not to Repeat the Sin

Obviously, all of this doesn't mean very much if you aren't sincerely committed not to sin again. This is the real expression of the fact that you have changed. Maimonides says that teshuva is complete when you reach a point that, when faced with exactly the same circumstances and temptations, you would make the right choice.

Does that answer your question?

Love,
Daniella

Teshuva

Jewish Symbols

Dear Josep,

I have a jewelry box a friend bought me while serving in Iraq for the US Army. One of the things that struck me when I saw it was the decorative motif that runs along the perimeter: a row of six-pointed stars.

What is a six-pointed star—widely known as the Jewish Star, the Star of David, or the Shield of David—doing on a box made by a Muslim in a country with virtually no Jews?

As it turns out, the association between the six-pointed star and Judaism is a fairly recent one. The same shape was a popular decoration motif in the Middle Ages and it could be found in churches and mosques as well as in synagogues. It's not clear why it became associated with Jews, or why we began to refer to it as the Shield of David (*Magen David*). It has been a Kabbalistic symbol since the 16th century, sometimes called the Seal of Solomon. Some think it became associated specifically with Jews because of the patches we were forced to wear in the late Middle Ages, which were sometimes shaped something like the six-pointed star. (In Spain, before the expulsion, it was a red circle.) In the 17th century, it appeared on synagogues, probably used the same way crosses were used to identify Christian places of worship. At any rate, it was only in the late 19th century that the Star of David became a universally accepted Jewish symbol—when the Zionist movement adopted it. Apparently there was some controversy over using it as the symbol in the center of the flag of the State of Israel.

In any case, as you know, today it is exclusively associated with Jews, and a popular motif for clothing or jewelry expressing Jewish identity.

As I've mentioned, the original symbol of Jews was not the Star of David, but the menorah—the seven-branched candelabra that was lit in the Temple. It is that symbol that is displayed on the Arch of Titus to identify the slaves portrayed there as Judeans. That's why it was chosen as the centerpiece of the emblem of the State of Israel.

Another symbol commonly associated with Jews is the *chamsa*. It's the shape of a hand. Actually, it's a widely used symbol of good luck in the Middle East and North Africa, and not exclusively for Jews. The right hand is a positive symbol in many cultures. Jews, in particular, associate the five fingers with experiencing God with the five senses, or the five books of the Torah. The word "chamsa" means "five" in Arabic.

A more exclusively Jewish symbol is the word חי, *chai*, which means "live." In Hebrew, each letter corresponds to a number. The numerical value of the letters ח and י is eighteen, so eighteen is considered an auspicious number and Jews often give gift money or charity in multiples of eighteen. As you know, Jews love life, and the typical Jewish toast is *L'chaim*—"To life!"

We also often use other Hebrew writing—quotes from the Tanakh or from rabbinic writings—as decoration. You can see this on the walls of many ancient (and modern) synagogues.

Another symbol commonly found on Jewish buildings is the Tablets of the Covenant. Usually they appear rounded on top... not sure why. They usually either have the first ten Hebrew letters representing the Ten Commandments, or the first two or three words of each commandment.

And the last symbol I will mention here, is the *Choshen*. That was the special breastplate worn by the High Priest in the days of the Temple, which had twelve precious stones, each stone representing one of the Twelve Tribes. Its meaning and significance are obscure, but seems to have something to do with atonement and judgement.

All these symbols are incorporated into our decor, jewelry, or household items, and can be found pretty much everywhere in Israel.

Love,
Daniella

Jewish Symbols

The Sabbath Keeps the Jews...
Even When It Seems like It Doesn't

Dear Josep,

As you know, we had some seriously crazy weather over the weekend. And this time the title "Snowpocalypse" is not nearly as ironic and silly as it was when we used it to describe the snowstorm in January. This one was the worst and coldest storm in modern Israeli history. We're talking over half a meter of snow (about two feet) in Jerusalem, and even more at higher elevations, in Judea, Samaria, and the North. Haifa got snow for the first time in twenty-two years. This part of the country was in total lockdown, and, to make matters worse, damage from the winds caused a lot of disruption in electricity supply so tens of thousands of people were without power during the coldest nights of the year. Thousands of people had to be rescued and evacuated, emergency shelters were set up, the Israel Electric Company declared a state of national emergency... total chaos.

And if that doesn't sound bad enough, the worst of it had to be on Friday evening. We had no power for two-and-a-half hours before Shabbat, making Shabbat preparations difficult, to say the least. The power—mercifully—came back on very low tension just long enough before Shabbat for me to take a warm shower and for us to enjoy a warm and well-lit evening meal with our neighbors. Shortly after we came back upstairs to put the little one to bed, the power went out again, and stayed off for about eighteen hours.

Did I mention that all our heating devices run on electricity? And that we're not allowed to light fires or turn on any electric devices (including battery-powered ones) on Shabbat—except in life-threatening situations?

If you're wondering how cold it was, let's just say our milk didn't spoil even though the refrigerator was off for thirty-six hours.

We were okay overall, and the kids were mostly happy in several layers of clothing, though they kept waking up during the night because of the dark and cold and forcing us to climb out from under all our blankets to calm them. I was the most miserable of all of us. What can I do? I'm used to Shabbat being about festivity and warm food and good company and good cheer. All four were significantly missing during the day as we struggled to stay warm and keep the kids from going crazy. We were supposed to have a guest over for lunch, but she understandably stayed under her blankets. Eitan delivered some food to her when we finished eating, for which she was very grateful.

We didn't even get to play in the measly inch or so of snow we got out here by the desert, because we had no way to get warm afterwards!

Concerning the commandment to keep the Sabbath, God said, *"Between Me and the People of Israel it shall be an eternal sign."* (Exodus 31:17) Lighting the candles to signify the beginning of Shabbat always gives me the sense of "handing it all over to Him," knowing that now He is taking over, I have no more control, and I'm keeping Shabbat as a sign of my love for Him and trust in Him. This Friday, I was strongly reminded of the sense of extreme vulnerability—and helpless sort of hope—that I felt when I lit the candles through the cracked open, chained door to the balcony in the youth hostel in Barcelona seven years ago;[44] the same sense of, "Well, I have no idea how

---

[44] See *How It All Began*.

this is going to turn out, but God, I'm just going to have to trust You." The electricity was still on at the time, but we knew it might turn off any moment, and I just felt so grateful to have my shower and warm food waiting for us. Tears welled in my eyes as I watched the snow flutter down outside the window where our candles glowed. My four-year-old asked me what I was doing. I said I was watching the snow. He asked why. I said, "Because it's beautiful." I put my arm around him and said, "You know... God is always telling us that He loves us. He tells us all the time, by constantly giving to us. Keeping Shabbat is our way of telling Him that we love Him back."

On the list of Most Challenging Shabbatot Ever, this one definitely outranks the one in Barcelona. (For goodness' sake, maybe I was hungry and upset, but at least I was warm, there was Ben & Jerry's involved, and I didn't have screaming kids to deal with!) I spent most of the time without power being cold, desperate, and miserable. You know what? Being a Jew is hard. It means being totally committed to an intense and sometimes very demanding relationship with Someone whose communication with you is often very hard to interpret or even notice, and who very often doesn't answer your requests in the way you would like or ultimately think is "right." But at the end of the day, I know that it's worth it. I know that He knows what He is doing better than I do. And I know He's really looking out for me, and giving me what I need—just enough pain and suffering for me to learn and grow, and more nurturing and abundance and goodness than I sometimes know what to do with. I don't always get it, and sometimes I get angry, but as with all the relationships I've been reflecting on in the last couple of years, I'm learning that anger and disappointment are inherent and indispensable parts of a deep and meaningful relationship with someone, and not only do they not destroy everything, sometimes they can even have constructive power.

There's an old saying that more than the Jews keep the Sabbath, the Sabbath keeps the Jews. I used to understand this to mean that the magical atmosphere and time to focus on what's important—our relationships with God, our families and our friends—is what gave us strength to face each difficult week throughout the centuries. But I think it's more than that. Some Shabbatot are neither magical nor joyous. Some mitzvot are very hard to follow. At the end of the day, our willingness to stay committed, despite how difficult it is, can bring us closer to Him, and Him closer to us. It's an eternal sign between us. Most times, it's a bed of petals. Occasionally, it's a bed of thorns. Ultimately, it is all roses.

Love,
Daniella

Links in the Chain:
On Educating Children

Dear Josep,

    I remember you telling me once that one of the things you liked about Jews and Judaism was the strong emphasis on education and love of learning. Jewish literacy rates were always significantly higher than those of the surrounding populations, and it all comes down to the fact that teaching our children is one of the most important commandments in the Torah. Combine that with the love of delving into the depths of the Torah that characterized our ancestors, and it's no wonder that there's a completely out-of-the-park disproportionate representation of Jews in the sciences and other fields that require a lot of study.

    As with everything, the Sages guide us in how to properly educate our children and raise them to serve God and be good Jews and good people.

    You asked me last year about two things that stood out to you about my kids. The first was their *payot*—their sidecurls. The other was their *tzitziyot*, the four-cornered garment worn underneath the shirt with fringes on each corner.

    When you see a Jewish boy with these things, he's probably over three years old. Why? Because age three is what we call *gil chinukh*—the "age of education." It's when we start teaching them about the Torah and the mitzvot. There's a custom to let their hair grow out until the third birthday, so that we can cut it on that day to teach them about the mitzvah of payot; the prohibition to shave that area above and behind the ears to create a rounded shape—because this was a symbol of idolatrous practices back in the day. (The payot don't need to be that long, but like with beards, growing them out is an outward symbol of piety.) We also have them start wearing tzitziyot and kippot at this age. These are all highly visual and experiential mitzvot that make the children look and feel different, and that's why they're the best ones to start with.

The mitzvah of tzitzit is sourced in the third section of the Shema prayer:

Speak to the children of Israel, and tell them that they make, throughout their generations, fringes in the corners of their garments, and that they put with the fringe of each corner a thread of blue. And it shall be unto you a fringe, so that you may look upon it, and remember all the commandments of the Lord, and do them; and so that you will not go about after your own heart and your own eyes, after which you go astray; so that you may remember and do all My commandments, and be holy unto your God.
(Numbers 15:38-40)

So the very idea of this commandment is that it is a visual reminder of God's presence... sort of the clothing version of the mezuzah.[45]

Kippot are actually not a Biblical commandment and even rabbinically they are only required when studying Torah or praying. The idea is modesty before God when speaking of Him. But, today, most observant Jewish men wear them all the time, and they have become an expression of Jewish identity, to a point where *not* wearing one is considered to be making a statement. So practically speaking, we think of it as a requirement.

---

[45] See *On the Doorposts of Your Homes: All About Mezuzot.*

Anyway, back to chinukh. Age three is also when we start teaching them to recite blessings and basic prayers, and to light candles for Shabbat. Observant Judaism is so complex and there are so many details, we don't try to teach it all at once; we introduce things slowly and organically. You probably don't remember when we were walking home from the playground on Shabbat and one of my kids picked up a coin from the ground; I mentioned that we're not allowed to carry money on Shabbat, and you asked if you should take it from him, and I said no. I don't want them to experience Shabbat as something restrictive and harsh, so I choose my battles carefully. Children are not obligated in mitzvot until their *bar* or *bat mitzvah*—at age twelve for girls and thirteen for boys. In Judaism, this is the age where they become morally responsible for themselves. By this age, of course, most of them have been keeping all the mitzvot for years, with the possible exception of fasting on fast days.

I was thinking about this lately as I listened to my sons recite the blessing over tzitzit in the morning. There's a concept in Yiddish and Hebrew that's not quite translatable into English, called *nachat* (or *naches* in Yiddish). It's that sense of contented joy and pride you get when your children or other loved ones live up to your hopes for them and "do you proud." That's what I feel when I hear the sweet voices of my children reciting that blessing. Slowly, carefully, I'm taking this precious gift passed down to me through hundreds of generations starting at Mount Sinai, and passing it on to my own children; becoming a link in the chain that roots us in the past and raises us toward the future.

Love,
Daniella

Links in the Chain

The Vagueries of the Jewish Afterlife

Dear Josep,

A number of years ago, you shared a highly amusing little Rowan Atkinson routine with me, where he pretends to be the Devil welcoming all the new arrivals to Hell. He goes through the various groups of people, and at one point says, "And finally... Christians. Christians? Ah, yes, I'm sorry, I'm afraid the Jews were right..."

I responded that Eitan and I had laughed our heads off at it, and then, "Of course, if [the Jews were indeed right], the whole thing would be set up very differently, and their term of stay in Hell would only last a year... but I don't expect Rowan Atkinson to know that."

You asked me to explain, and I responded, "I never told you about the Jewish concepts of the afterlife? Probably because they are vague, disputed, and overall a rather unimportant aspect of Judaism..." and proceeded to give a brief overview of the concepts of the Jewish afterlife with which I'm most familiar, by comparing it to the Christian concepts and pointing out the differences.

Today, I'm going to go more in depth.

From a theological perspective, the idea of the existence of an afterlife is a very simple answer to the problem of Divine justice. It explains how good people can suffer in this world,

The Vagueries of the Jewish Afterlife

by saying that justice will be served after we die. That's why it's such a crucial part of every religion. In Judaism, however, there's a notable lack of focus on the afterlife. I've always said that it's because Judaism is much more focused on this world, what to do in it and how to improve it, than on the next world.

In the Mishna (Ethics of the Fathers, 1:4) it says: *"Be not like a servant who serves his Master in order to receive a reward, but rather like a servant who serves his Master unconditionally."* Why would a servant serve his master unconditionally? Out of love, right? Love, and the sense that the service itself is the reward; and in cases where that doesn't feel true, the belief that the master has one's best interests at heart, and knows best, even when the servant doesn't understand. Eitan pointed out to me recently that we have so many more pressing things to focus on, that the afterlife is sort of an afterthought for us. Unlike its numerous mentions in the Christian Bible and in the Qur'an, only a few, very vague references to an afterlife exist in the Jewish Bible, and never in detail.

So do we believe in an afterlife? Yes, we do. For Jewish philosophers, too, it serves as an answer to the question of Divine justice. (Not the only one; but it's part of explaining how the world is more complex than what we see in front of us.) However, unlike in Christianity and Islam, the details of what it is, what it looks like, etc., are not part of our belief system and therefore are basically a topic of discussion and dispute rather than doctrine. So you'll find a very wide variety of opinions on it in rabbinical literature.

If you ask an observant Jew about his beliefs regarding the afterlife, he'll probably answer something like what I will describe below. These are the most mainstream views of it that exist in Torah observant Judaism. But again, it's important to emphasize that this is mostly speculation. The most accurate answer to the question of what the afterlife is according to Judaism, is: "We don't know. Now, let's talk about how to kasher that saucepan."

Olam HaBa/Gan Eden

We have two ways to refer to our version of Heaven: *Olam HaBa*, "the World to Come," and *Gan Eden*, "the Garden of Eden." The latter of those implies a return to our pre-Adam's-sin state of simplicity and oneness with God. But, unlike other religions that describe in great detail the pleasures that await a righteous person in Heaven, Judaism is very vague on this. In our prayer liturgy for the dead, we refer to basking in God's light, or sitting near His throne. We talk about one's soul being bound in the bond of life (*tzrura b'tzror hachaim*). I'm sure the Kabbalah has a lot to say about it, but Kabbalistic thought is not generally mainstream.

Basically, we don't really know what it is. All we know is that it's good, some kind of eternal peace, and we talk about there being some kind of hierarchy according to the spiritual level one achieved during his lifetime.

So how do we get there?

This is a very Christian question. A better question in Judaism is, how do we *not* get to Olam HaBa. The general assumption, and not just with Jews, but with every human being, is that he or she will take part in Olam HaBa. (It may involve a few steps to get there, upon which we'll elaborate in a moment.) You have to do something specifically wrong not to get there. In the Torah, there are a few commandments that list the punishment for transgressing them as *karet*. It is the harshest punishment in the Torah—even harsher than death. No one really knows what karet is, but the root k.r.t., כ.ר.ת., generally means "cut off," and a common interpretation of the term is that it means being cut off from the physical and spiritual world, meaning when that person dies, he or she simply ceases to exist. The soul is destroyed and does not live on. Do not pass Go, do not collect $200.[46]

---

[46] They *do* have Monopoly in Catalonia, right?

Gehennom

So this is the closest thing we have to Hell. But really, if we're comparing to Christian theology, it's more like what y'all call purgatory.

You see, in Christianity, Hell is permanent. If you're a sinner and/or you don't accept Jesus, you're condemned to an eternity of suffering. Fire and brimstone, etc.[47]

In Judaism, this is not so. Gehennom is a stage in a process of spiritual purification or cleansing. That process actually begins with the physical world, or at least, the parts of the process we are aware of. We see life as an opportunity to purify and refine our souls, by making the right choices in this life. If we have not managed to do so in this life, there are two possibilities, at least according to my own beliefs: Gehennom, and reincarnation, which we'll get to in a moment. So again, no one really knows what Gehennom is or what exactly happens there, but the most common explanation I've heard is that it's a state of remorse and regret for not living up to your full potential. It appears to be a state of understanding why the things you did wrong were wrong, how they affected you and those around you, and what you could have done and been versus what you did and were... and the subsequent profound regret that comes with that.

Our sources say that this process lasts as long as that individual soul needs, which is, at the *very* most, a year. That's why we recite Kaddish, the Mourner's Prayer, for a year after the death of a parent. Actually, we recite it only for eleven months, under the belief that no one could possibly be wicked enough to deserve the full twelve months.

When the process is complete and the soul is "cleansed," it then moves on to Olam HaBa.

In essence, Gehennom is actually not really a different place than Olam HaBa, but a part of it. Jew in the City (an Internet personality who, by the way, is also a great resource

---

[47] That's what awaits me according to your religion. Thanks a bunch.

for people looking to learn about the basic concepts of Judaism) has a cute video explaining how it's like the difference between attending a symphony as someone who has a deep appreciation for music and understanding of it, versus attending the same symphony as someone who hates classical music and has never even bothered to learn to appreciate it. For the first person, it's Heaven; for the second, it's Hell. Gehennom, in this allegory, is the place where at first the "music" is torture, but then you slowly learn to enjoy and appreciate it, and then it becomes Heaven for you.

Reincarnation

Not all Jews believe in reincarnation. As with all this stuff, it's opinion, not doctrine, and reincarnation even more so than the other things. Personally, as you know, I do believe in reincarnation; I believe it is another way to cleanse souls that, for whatever reason God decides, need to be purified this way and not through Gehennom. We come back to this world and live another life, completing whatever lessons we needed to learn or achievements we needed to accomplish in the previous lifetime, but did not.

Resurrection of the Dead

This concept is one that is specifically mentioned in our scriptures. It's not really about the afterlife, but about the Messianic Era. Our tradition teaches that when the Messiah comes, the righteous dead will come back to life to experience and take part in the Redemption of the World. Most of our Sages interpret this as being 100% literal. Most Jewish cemeteries all over the world are arranged with the graves facing Jerusalem, with the idea that when the dead are resurrected, they can just climb on out of the grave and conveniently find themselves facing the right direction.[48]

Obviously, this is a bit of a stretch for a rationalist like myself. I tend to prefer to take this as being metaphorical; after all, no one actually knows what the Messianic Age will look like either. In fact, the Messianic Age is also referred to as Olam HaBa in many sources, so there seems to be some idea there about the joining of the physical and spiritual world into one, and that makes a little more sense to me.

The Devil

So actually the concept of Satan in Judaism has nothing at all to do with the afterlife, but I'm bringing it up here to fully address Rowan Atkinson's routine. The word "Satan" means "adversary," and in Christian thought, the Devil is kind of God's enemy in that he tries to attract people to sin and therefore, I suppose, is appointed master of Hell, which is where the sinners go. In Christian thought, the Devil is a sort of independent force that works *against* God. In Jewish thought, Satan is a spiritual entity that works *for* God and is subordinate to Him. He (it...) is an "adversary" in that he is the 'prosecutor' against us in the Heavenly Court. (This is all allegorical.) He makes claims against us and is harsh on us, but he still works for the Judge and for justice. In a sense, Satan is kind of an externalized conception of the Evil Inclination, *yetzer hara*, the part of human nature that attracts man to sin.

In summary: here's hoping the Jews are, indeed, right on this one.

Love,
Daniella

---

[48] They might be a little disappointed to discover that the gates are locked.

The Battleground of Good and Evil

Dear Josep,
    One of the major philosophical differences I have noted between Christianity and Judaism is our concept of the nature of man, what he is capable of, and what he needs in order to elevate himself above the darker aspects of his nature.
    When I first encountered this difference, I was skeptical. I was educated from a strong Jewish perspective, so I was aware that anything anybody said about Christianity was sure to cast it in a negative light. Therefore, I thought that maybe those who had taught me about this aspect of Christianity had been exaggerating it. But the more I learned about the fundamental principles of Christianity, the more I realized that this difference does exist; and that maybe the fact that I see it as a negative aspect attests to how deeply ingrained the opposite idea is in my belief system.
    The root of the disagreement is in how we interpret the results of what Christians call the Original Sin, the sin of Adam and Eve.
    Both Christians and Jews agree that when Adam and Eve ate from the Tree of Knowledge, it fundamentally changed the nature of man, his purpose and goals, and the nature of the world in which he lived. We also both believe that the sin

The Battleground of Good and Evil

caused some kind of intermingling, or "tainting," of humankind with evil. But what Christians believe this means is that man can never redeem himself from his inherent evil; that it is part of his essence, from which he can never escape on his own. The only way to redeem oneself from it, Christianity says, is salvation through Christ. That is, that God manifested Himself in His son—Jesus—who then suffered and died on the cross to atone for that original sin. All you have to do to redeem yourself from evil, then, is to accept Jesus. (Obviously, different streams of Christianity have different ideas about exactly how to do that and what it means, but that's the basic idea.) That way, God will grant you salvation and grace.

It took me years and a lot of reading to fully wrap my head around that concept, because it's just so foreign to me.

So here's what Jews believe about the sin of Adam and Eve.

The Tree of Knowledge is actually not exactly an accurate translation of what the tree is called in Genesis. In the text, it is called "עץ הדעת טוב ורע," "the Tree of the Knowledge of Good and Evil." But the word for "knowledge," "דעת," does not simply mean "knowledge" as in wisdom, awareness, understanding, or the retention of information. "דעת" implies a deep intermingling, synthesis, and connection. When the Torah says a man "knew" his wife and then she became pregnant, it's not just a euphemism; "knowledge" in that context is describing a deep connection. A more accurate translation of the name of the tree, then, would be "**the Tree of the Synthesis of Good and Evil.**"

So the effect of the Tree of the Synthesis of Good and Evil was not simply to give man "knowledge," but to cause an intertwining of good and evil within man. Before eating from the fruit of the Tree, evil did not exist within man. It was embodied in the snake, which was an external source of doubt and rebellion against God.

In Judaism, we have a concept of the "good inclination" and the "evil inclination"—*yetzer tov* and *yetzer ra* respectively. This is what we call these opposite forces that exist within us, the yetzer tov pulling us to strive for Godliness, and the yetzer

267

ra pulling us to toward our base desires. We believe that man lives with a constant conflict between these inclinations. The real essence of our soul, our higher self, is really the yetzer tov; that is how God originally created us. The yetzer ra was the result of Adam and Eve eating the fruit of the Tree. It was no longer externalized as the snake. It became an integral part of the nature of Adam and Eve when they ate the fruit.

Our goal, our purpose, in life and in the world, is to overcome the yetzer ra, first within ourselves, and then outside ourselves, in the world at large. We believe that man is capable of this—that, indeed, this is the mission God endowed us as people and especially as Jews. We do not need God's salvation to overcome the evil within us, Judaism says. It is a constant struggle, but we believe that our job is to do it ourselves.

That said, God does help us out in a number of ways. The most important way, according to Judaism, was the giving of the Torah. The Torah is essentially a guidebook on overcoming the yetzer ra on a personal and societal level, and that is really the purpose of the mitzvot—to help us attain that goal. That's why the Torah is represented in the Garden of Eden, and later symbolically referred to, as the Tree of Life. **The "fruits" of the Torah—the mitzvot—are the antidote to the fruits of the Tree of the Synthesis of Good and Evil.**

Jews and Christians agree that there were additional punishments God gave Adam and Eve because of their sin. He banished them from the Garden of Eden; he made them mortal; he cursed both Adam and Eve with the difficulty of labor—Adam laboring for bread, and Eve laboring for children. My interpretation of the significance of these punishments is that they were direct consequences of the synthesis of good and evil within man. God created the world in order to bestow His goodness upon it. But now, because good and evil were hopelessly intertwined, man would have to work hard to overcome the evil and attain the Godliness that he was created to receive. He could no longer sit in paradise and bask in God's light. He needed to search for it and work for it, in a world where it was no longer obvious and tangible.

The Battleground of Good and Evil

While this sounds like quite a bummer, Rabbi Aryeh Kaplan points something out in his work, *A World of Love*, which reveals the unique power of a world in which good and evil can mingle. In the spiritual world, he says, proximity is determined by similarity. That is, if we wish to become close to God spiritually, we must become more like Him. The less we are like Him, the farther away from Him we are. By that understanding, in the spiritual world, nothing could possibly be farther away from good than evil. They are completely opposite and therefore can never engage with one another.

But spiritual matter can be anchored to physical matter—such as a soul to a body. And in the physical world, things that are evil can exist in very close proximity to things that are good. In that sense, then, this world, in which good and evil intermingle, is the only place where good can overcome evil. Our world is sort of a battleground between these two opposite forces, and we human beings are the soldiers on either side; it's up to us to choose which side. This battle wages within our hearts, but, as you can clearly see, it also wages fiercely outside us, between different groups of humans who are making different choices about how to relate to the good and evil within themselves.

If you're interested in exploring these ideas more deeply, I highly recommend giving *A World of Love* a slow and careful read.

But for now, back to human nature according to Judaism and Christianity.

I was inspired to write about this by an article on the Internet about Dr. Viktor Frankl. Now, if you've never heard of this man or his iconic work, *Man's Search for Meaning*... well, then, I don't even know what to do with you because if anyone on Earth should have read that book, it's you! Dr. Viktor Frankl was a Jewish Austrian psychiatrist who survived Auschwitz. *Man's Search for Meaning* chronicles Dr. Frankl's experiences in the concentration camp with a focus on his observations regarding the effect of the inmates' attitudes on their survival, and goes on to describe the psychotherapeutic method he developed as a result of his observations, which he called "logotherapy." His overarching idea is that, more than anything else, man strives for a sense of purpose and meaning to his life, and that when he feels that his life has meaning, he can withstand even the most horrific conditions. And no one is more qualified than a survivor of Auschwitz to attest to that.

Seriously. If you haven't read it, get on that, pronto. [49]

Anyway, the article I mentioned brought a five-minute video excerpt from a lecture of Dr. Frankl's, in which he says, "If we take man as he really is, we make him worse. But if we overestimate him… we promote him to what he really can be. So we have to be idealists, in a way—because then we wind up as the true, the real realists."

No wonder the Nazis tried to get rid of him. What a quintessentially Jewish idea.

Humans are not static; we're constantly evolving. You can't give a precise measurement of a person's goodness or potential, because these things are in constant flux. And when we believe in each other and in ourselves, believe that we are all capable of being better than we currently are, we create a supportive reality for ourselves to actually attain that potential. In essence, he's saying that the higher our expectations and hopes for ourselves, the higher we can reach.

That is why I find the Christian concept of the Original Sin and the inherent sinfulness of man so discouraging. Because in a sense, Christianity is telling us that we cannot make ourselves more than we are; only God can do that. And I much prefer to believe that I have the ability to overcome my darker nature and become a better person. But I can see something comforting in the Christian idea, too. When you don't have the capacity to redeem yourself of sin, you don't have that responsibility, either. You can (and indeed, must) hand it over to

---

[49] Josep wishes to register his indignation at the mere suggestion in this letter that he may not have read *Man's Search for Meaning*. It was required reading at school right around the time he saw *Schindler's List*, and he found it an emotionally harrowing read.

the priest, or to Jesus, or to God. We Jews don't have that option. We have to take full responsibility for ourselves and our natures. A rabbi can only council us, he can't absolve us of sin. God will only cleanse us of sin if we're willing to change ourselves, as I explained in my letter on teshuva. We must constantly struggle, believing that we have the capacity to overcome. This (among many other things!) makes Judaism a much more challenging and demanding approach to life. And, obviously, I'm totally biased, but in my view, it's well worth it. The reward of achieving something you've worked for is sweeter than any gift someone could give you.

Much love,
Daniella

Crossing Boundaries

Dear Josep,

So I have to tell you a story.

Yesterday, my eldest son wore one of the Barcelona soccer team shirts you gave us. The kids wear them frequently.

There was a substitute teacher at his kindergarten yesterday, someone who's not usually part of the staff and hadn't seen him wearing one of the shirts before. She noticed something about it that I hadn't: the upper left section of the FCB symbol is a St. George's cross.[50]

Hmm... is this a problem, you ask? Well, not exactly. It's the same symbol that appears on the Swiss flag, and the British flag, and, you know, the Red Cross and all. Religious symbols that are used in what is very clearly a non-religious context are okay according to Jewish law. (Some may argue that sport is a religion in and of itself, but let's not get into that!)

There are, however, those who feel that there is inherent... um... negativity in certain symbols, such as the cross, and that they have a negative spiritual influence on those who wear them or come in contact with them. So this substitute teacher is apparently one of those people.

---

[50] St. George (St. Jordi in Catalan) is the patron saint of Catalonia. St. Jordi's Day is widely celebrated in Catalonia. See *A Little Catalan Context*.

Now before I go on, full disclosure: I am also fairly uncomfortable around Christian symbols. As my activities of the past couple years and my Facebook friends list testify, I have gotten a lot more comfortable with interacting with other faiths. My reaction was more of amusement than discomfort when we arrived at our beach rental in Florida and discovered that our hosts had graciously provided for all our physical and spiritual needs, in the form of crucifixes and a painting of Mary on the walls. Still, I'm a Jew, and here's a shocker: I don't believe in Jesus. Moreover, the crucifix has been a symbol of persecution of my people through much of history, and its spiritual significance does not speak to me, to say the least. I do believe, to some degree, in the power of symbols, much like I believe in the power of words. And much as I may respect Christians and Christianity, I'm not a Christian and proper boundaries must be established. We discreetly took down the crucifix in the kids' room and put it back up when we left. We decided Mary could stay in our bedroom, 'cause, you know, whatever, it's just a painting of a lady.

A nice Jewish lady.

Anyway, the substitute teacher. So apparently she, like our hosts in Florida, felt a personal responsibility for my son's soul, and proceeded to explain to him that it's very bad for a Jew to wear that symbol, and then to tell him a story that involved a famous Jewish rabbi, Rabbi Mordekhai Eliyahu, not letting someone into his hospital room because there was a small cross shape on the tag of his shirt. That story was relayed to us later by my son in the following manner: there was somebody who wanted to go into the hospital, but they wouldn't let him, because he was wearing a symbol of the *goyim* (gentiles).

...

I sent a very stern message to the main kindergarten teacher (not yet knowing that it was the substitute who had told him this), that read: "I would have appreciated it if you had spoken to me about my son's shirt rather than relaying the message through him. The shirt was a gift from a dear friend of mine who lives in Barcelona, and I hadn't even noticed that there was a cross on it... We educate our children to respect every person regardless of religion, race, or gender, and that shirt is actually very important to me in the context of educating my son in respect and appreciation of people who are not Jewish."

The teacher responded with bewilderment, and after some discussion, it became clear that it was the substitute who'd had this conversation with him. The teacher took this very seriously. She thanked me for telling her and spoke with the substitute. The latter then called me and proceeded to give me the following non-apology:

"You're absolutely right, I should have said it to you and not through him, but what can I say... it just came out... apparently from God... you see, your son is so special, he's really a very elevated soul, I see how he speaks and his beautiful drawings, there's really something very special about him, and my heart hurts for him and all the difficulties he's had. It's because of his elevated soul that these difficulties are attracted to him, you know? So I saw that shirt with the symbol, and you know, it's such a strong symbol, and Rabbi Mordekhai Eliyahu writes about how much negative influence this symbol can have... I asked him about the shirt and he said, I don't know, something about an uncle or something who lives in Spain..." (You've been upgraded to uncle! Congratulations!) She then proceeded to explain to me about the actual version of the story she had told him. "If he were my child, I'd be so careful about things like this... but I know, he's your child, and maybe you don't believe in such things. But it was like when you see a child running into the street, and even if he's not your child, you just have to shout at him to get out of the street..."

Through gritted teeth, I thanked her for her concern and her appreciation of my son, and repeated again that she should have mentioned it to me and not to him, and that she should think about the effect stories like that might have on him, since it seems to have scared and upset him a little. I explained to her as well, though I know it would probably scandalize her, about my philosophy of educating for tolerance... and about the identity of the giver of the shirt. (People who are familiar with the norms of my community don't even know what to do with me telling them that I have a "dear friend" who is non-Jewish, male, and from Spain. Too bad she was on the phone so I couldn't see her face.)

The permanent staff of the kindergarten responded with utmost seriousness and professionalism to the incident. The main teacher told me that the staff discussed it and is going to meet with all the teachers including the substitutes to clarify the professional boundaries of the classroom.

The funny thing is, Josep, that if it had had nothing to do with you, I probably would have just sort of rolled my eyes and beneath the exasperation and indignation that this woman had the gall to undermine the education of my child, I might have even felt a little admiration for her devotion. Part of my whole "interfaith" thing is that I have a kind of soft spot for people who are extremely devoted to their faith and who maintain a spiritual awareness at all times. But because that shirt was a gift from you, and is important to me—obviously, not just in the context of education—for that reason... boy, did she strike a nerve! When my son reported the incident I got *so* angry, to the point that Eitan had to talk me down a little and remind me that I was speaking to my almost-six-year-old child.

Eitan blacked out the cross on the shirt with a permanent marker. I had mixed feelings about him doing anything to it, and I really hope it doesn't upset or offend you. You should know that I treasure all the gifts you have given us—physical and spiritual.[51]

Much love,
Daniella

---

[51] Just so you know—the black marker quickly faded in the laundry.

I Forgave God

Dear Josep,

As you and I have discussed recently, I have been experiencing a struggle in my relationship with God in the last number of years. There are many factors that played into this. Some were related to my own maturation and the deepening of the complexity in my understanding of what He is and is not. Some were the result of encounters with life situations, or with issues directly related to the Torah that sent me into something of a tailspin—having explanations that satisfied me intellectually, but not emotionally. As you can imagine, current events have brought that struggle to the forefront, and I find myself asking that same question, that ultimate question all people of faith struggle with again and again, phrased by Abraham when facing the destruction of Sodom: "Shall the Judge of all the Earth not act justly?" *Why do good people suffer?* Why does the all-powerful God choose not to intervene to protect the innocent?

If there's one thing I've been consistently learning in the past few years, it's how much of the distance and suffering I've felt in all relationships in my life come from suppressing and denying anger I feel toward the other. And how much can be repaired by simply giving space to that anger, and forgiving myself for having it and the other for triggering it (whether it was their fault or not).

You see, it's not that hard for me to acknowledge my anger and forgive someone who has hurt me, either intentionally or unintentionally, when he or she did something wrong. It's much harder for me to give space to my anger when it feels unjustified. Because what do I want from them? It wasn't their fault, what right do I have to be angry? I'm learning, however, that feelings don't work that way. They're not rational and don't respond to reason. I can't make my anger go away by simply telling it that it doesn't make sense. So it's all right to feel anger, even when the object of my anger truly did nothing wrong. You can't choose what you feel. You can only choose how to respond. And when I choose to respond by suppressing and denying anger, it doesn't actually disappear; it expresses itself in other, less healthy ways. It's a question of how the anger can be given space in a way that's healthy, with trust on both ends that it won't spell the destruction of the relationship. We get angry, we forgive each other, and we move on.

And the truth is that I get angry at God. I get furious with Him. Yes, I believe everything He does is for the ultimate good... but why does it have to hurt so much? God is all-powerful; couldn't He have created a world where suffering was *not* necessary? Yes, yes, I've studied all the well-known Jewish sources that address this deep question; I know that God created the world as an act of His love, and that love is about giving, and God wanted to bestow the ultimate good on the world, and that the ultimate good is God himself, and in order for Him to do this, He needed to give us free will, and there can be no free will without the existence of evil to choose against. But He is still all-powerful and this arrangement of the spiritual universe is all His creation; couldn't He have changed it so suffering wasn't necessary?

There's a debate in the Talmud between the two great schools, Beit Hillel and Beit Shammai, on whether it was easier for man to have been created, or not to have been created at all. They both agree in the end that it would have been easier for man *not* to have been created. From my vantage point, here in the Middle East in these days of instability, violence, and despair, this conclusion seems clear. Thanks a bunch, God, for all this ultimate goodness stuff, but really, I'd rather have nothing than to have to tolerate and witness so much suffering.

And that kind of thinking made me feel so ashamed of my lack of gratitude. God gave me so much, blessed me with so many wonderful things, and this is how I thank Him, by wishing He'd never created the world in the first place? Don't I believe He knows what He's doing? How could I possibly be angry at Him?

Something in that magic, soul-cleansing power of the High Holiday season, however, opened up a path for me. I realized that I needed to accept that it was okay for me to be angry. God may have made the world to bestow His ultimate goodness on it, but He also made us with a limited capacity to see and understand His plan, precisely so we wouldn't remain complacent in the face of injustice. Didn't God name our forefather Jacob, and our entire nation after him, "Israel"—"He who struggles with God"?

So I started letting myself be angry—and expressing that anger. For many years, I haven't really been speaking to Him freely the way I used to. I was *brogez*, to use the childish term from Israeli kindergartens for not being on speaking terms. I understood that my silence was not constructive; that it was better to spew anger at Him than to say nothing at all. So I started speaking my mind. Even when all I could say was, "Why are You doing this to me?" Even when it was something petty and inconsequential. I know that God cares about everything more deeply than I could possibly understand. There is no such thing as pain so small that it doesn't matter to Him.

On a Thursday night during Succot, we received the tragic news of that horrible terror attack in Samaria in which a young Jewish couple was murdered by terrorists right in front of their four little children. It was especially difficult because the couple was pretty well-known in the religious community, and I know several people who knew them personally. After Shabbat, we received more awful news—two Jews stabbed to death in the Old City of Jerusalem, the wife and two-year-old child of one of them injured and in the hospital. (As I've mentioned, the situation has only deteriorated since.) Naturally, I was very upset about these things, and started to feel the crushing fear of yet another escalation in violence and what it might mean for us. I wrote in a previous entry about the concept of "chosenness." I felt anger and despair over the persecution that seemed to be built into that role. Why, why, why? Why does being Jewish have to entail such constant suffering?

But then, on Simchat Torah, I stood in front of the ark (the cabinet where the Torah scrolls are kept) and read out the passages we recite before taking the Torah scrolls out and dancing with them. And I remembered that, as much as being Jewish entails constant suffering, it also entails so much of the deepest joy. As I danced with the Torah scroll, hugging it to my heart, offering it to my kids to kiss, I felt the profoundest sense of purpose and mission, and that brought me such elation. And I looked into my heart and suddenly saw something there I hadn't seen in a long time. I didn't feel that I was struggling *against* God. I felt that I was struggling *with* Him—*together with Him*. That even these terrible tragedies and this awful suffering was part of His plan for ultimate good, and that it was really for my good too, even if I couldn't see it. And that by taking part in this mission He gave to the Jewish people, I was partnering with Him in the act of bringing the world to a place where He will one day be able to bestow His ultimate good.

And I realized that I had forgiven Him for the pain He causes me.

Months ago, I read an intriguing article by Rabbi Ari Kahn about the period between Holocaust Remembrance Day and Israeli Independence Day (or, as I call it, Israeli Emotional Roller Coaster Week) in which he talks about the Talmudic commentary on God's instructions for the Temple sacrifices on Rosh Chodesh, the first day of the new month. He writes that we are commanded to bring what the Torah calls a "sin-offering" (*chata'at*) on Rosh Chodesh, but unlike every other time we're commanded to bring this type of offering, there's no sin listed that we are atoning for. The Talmud explains that God asks for a sin-offering on Rosh Chodesh, not as an atonement for a sin of ours, but a "sin" of *His*—the "sin" of diminishing the moon.[52]

Now obviously, this is not literal. God does not commit sins, and diminishing the moon seems to be a silly thing to be apologizing for. But there's a deep allegory here. The Jewish people is often compared to the moon, its phases representing the ups and downs we have experienced throughout our turbulent history. In Judaism, we talk about God "hiding His face," referring to times of great darkness and evil, where His goodness is not easily found. In contrast, there are times of "revelation," when it's much easier to see His hand in the events that are transpiring around us. The thing about the phases of the moon is that it *looks* like the moon is waxing and waning, growing and shrinking, appearing and disappearing. But it isn't. The moon remains exactly the same. The phases are an illusion, a trick of the light.

What the Talmud is saying is that God created the world exactly the way He wanted in exactly the ideal way. And He knows that the moon is always there. On Rosh Chodesh, He apologizes for the trick of the light, for the illusion that we humans perceive as the waxing and waning of the moon. He's asking us to forgive Him for hiding Himself from us without helping us understand why He does this. He does it because it is really for our ultimate good, but He knows we can't know or experience that. So He asks our forgiveness for the pain of the illusion of darkness.

When I read that article, I was floored. The concept of "forgiving God" seemed crazy and radical. *We* are the ones who are supposed to be asking for forgiveness! *We* are the ones who

---

[52] "And God said I am sorry," Rabbi Ari Kahn, *The Times of Israel* Blogs, April 28th, 2014.

are imperfect and are constantly falling short of our potential and making bad choices! God is just doing His job! He is the very definition of all that is right and true! How on earth could we have the arrogance to think there was any need forgive Him?

But now I understand. It isn't God who needs our forgiveness. It is we who need to allow ourselves to forgive Him. And to forgive ourselves for feeling anger and despair when He hides His face.

And when I remembered that article, I realized that God was hearing my anger, and asking me to forgive Him. I still don't understand, and the darkness still hurts. But knowing He knows my pain and "wishes" it was not necessary helps me feel that we're on the same page.

So I forgave God. And He forgave me. And something, some wound that has been festering in my soul for years, seems to have started to heal.

Love,
Daniella

Appendices

A Little Catalan Context

INDIVIDUALS UNFAMILIAR with the history and culture of the Iberian Peninsula may be very confused as to why I am constantly referring to Josep's culture as being "Catalan" as opposed to Spanish. When I first traveled to Barcelona I, too, had never heard of Catalan as a language or culture. Josep very quickly straightened me out! And seeing as I dedicated this entire book to explaining my own culture, I figure it is only fair to dedicate at least an appendix to Josep's culture. (Yes, one little appendix. Write your own book, Josep!)

So here's the story: Catalonia is, as of the moment I write these words, an autonomous region in northeastern Spain. I specify because there is currently a strong movement to secede from Spain and become an independent country by the year 2017. Historically, that region and some of the neighboring areas were first united under the Count of Barcelona. The County unified dynastically with the Kingdom of Aragon in the twelfth century, and ruled over Aragonese territory for the next seven centuries. However, it maintained a political structure, culture, and language distinct from those of Aragon, and became known as Catalonia. In the eighteenth century it was conquered by Castile, and has been under Spanish rule since. The Catalans have nonetheless maintained their unique culture, language, and identity.

Catalans have two cultural traditions that are noteworthy, one of which is mentioned a few times in the letters. That one is *El Caga-tió*, the Christmas log that "poops" out candy and gifts when children hit it with sticks. (Don't ask me, I just work here.) Josep sent me a video about this bizarre tradition a couple months after we met; I posted it on the blog in honor of Christmas 2014.[53]

---

[53] You can see that post at: letterstojosep.com/2014/12/24/and-now-for-something-a-little-different/

The other noteworthy cultural tradition is the celebration of St. Jordi's Day (April 23rd). Jordi is the Catalan form of the name George, and St. George is the patron saint of Catalonia. The holiday has become a sort of Catalan St. Valentine's Day, with lovers and friends exchanging roses (in honor of St. Jordi) and books (in honor of Shakespeare and Cervantes, who both died on April 23rd). I posted about this, too, in honor of St. Jordi's Day 2015.[54]

---

[54] letterstojosep.com/2015/4/23/st-jordis-day

Acknowledgements

FIRST AND FOREMOST, I must thank the First and Foremost, Master of the Universe, for everything. Like, literally everything.

As far as humans go, I'd have to be a special kind of ingrate not to thank Josep; this book would obviously never have existed without him! Many thanks to my husband and best friend, Eitan; my parents by birth and by love, my biggest supporters in every sense, Jeffrey & Jill Shames, and Mark & Nisa Levy; my #1 fan and unpaid publicist, Abi Levitt; my sister, Yonit Shames, who always believed in me; my brother-in-law, Ben Zhuk, and Jo Levitt, for their advice on books and publishing; and all others who gave me support, encouragement, and feedback. I would never have had the courage to do this without all of you.

Glossary

Aliyah: Immigration to Israel. Literally means "moving up." (May also refer to being called up to the Torah when it is read during services.)

Ashkenazi: Jews of central or eastern European descent. Around 80% of Jews today are Ashkenazi—including me. (See: *Different Kinds of Jews, Part I*.)

Brit or bris: Short for *brit milah*, literally the "covenant of circumcision." Usually refers to the circumcision ceremony that is performed on Jewish baby boys when they are eight days old. (See: *Circumcision. Wait! Don't Run Away Screaming!*)

Crypto-Judaism: The practice of Judaism in secret while publicly professing another faith. This phenomenon was particularly widespread in Spain after the riots of 1391, during which dozens, if not hundreds of thousands, of Jews were massacred and forcibly converted. These events put an end to the Jewish community in Barcelona until modern times.

Conversos: The Spanish term for converts to Christianity. They were also called *cristianos nuevos*, "New Christians."

Halakha: Jewish law.

Hashem: Literally "The Name" in Hebrew, this is how religious Jews often refer to God.

Goy: Non-Jew. The term is unfortunately sometimes used derogatorily, but I use it affectionately!

Kaddish: A special Jewish prayer in Aramaic. (See: *Processing Grief: Jewish Mourning Customs*.)

Kosher: Prepared according to the Jewish dietary laws (called **kashrut**). (See: *Jew Food, Parts I, II, and III*.)

Kiddush: Literally "sanctification." A ceremony performed over wine that is a "declaration" of the holiness of the day (on the Sabbath and holidays).

Kippah: A special cap traditionally worn by Jewish men.

Marranos: The same as Conversos, except that this was a derogatory term that literally means "swine." Today, it has lost its derogatory connotation, but I still prefer not to use it.

Mezuzah (plural: mezuzot): A little scroll, usually stored in a decorative protective case, that Jews affix to the doorposts of their homes. (See: *On the Doorposts of Your Home: All About Mezuzot*.)

Minyan: A quorum of ten men required for prayer.

Mitzvah: Commandment. (Plural: mitzvot.)

Mitzvot HaTluyot Ba'Aretz: Commandments associated with the Land of Israel.

Sephardi/Sephardic: Jews of Iberian origin. The definition is often expanded to include North African, Middle Eastern, and Asian Jewish communities, since the character of those communities was strongly influenced by Spanish Jews who arrived in those places after the expulsion of 1492; or because their customs tend to be more like those of Sephardi Jews than those of Ashkenazi Jews. (See: *Different Kinds of Jews, Part I*.)

Glossary

Shabbat: The Jewish Sabbath, which begins on Friday at sundown and ends Saturday evening after the stars emerge. (Also pronounced *Shabbos*. I use the Sephardi/Israeli pronunciation in Hebrew. *Shabbos* is the Ashkenazi pronunciation.) (See: *Shabbat: A Sacred Space in Time.*)

Shechita: The practice of kosher slaughter. (See: *Jew Food, Part 1.*)

Shema: The Shema prayer is a prayer that is central to Judaism. (See: *On the Doorposts of Your Home: All About Mezuzot.*)

Shiva: Literally "seven." The seven days of mourning after the death of a close family member. (See: *Processing Grief: Jewish Mourning Customs.*)

Shochet: A ritual slaughterer. (See: *Jew Food, Part I.*)

The Talmud: A compilation of what used to be the Oral Law, including the **Mishna** and the **Gemara**. It is second only to the Bible in terms of its importance in Judaism. (See: *An Introduction to the World's Biggest Book Club.*)

The Temple: The Holy Temple in Jerusalem was the center of Jewish ritual worship for hundreds of years. It was destroyed by the Babylonians, rebuilt seventy years later, and then destroyed again by the Romans. The remaining vestige, the western retaining wall (also known as the Western Wall, the Wailing Wall, or the Kotel) has been the most important site of Jewish prayer since the destruction of the Second Temple. For more information on the Temple and its importance in Judaism, see *Why Jerusalem Matters* and *Between the Dire Straits.*

The Torah: This term may refer specifically to the first Five Books of Moses in the Bible (the Pentateuch), or to the entire set of laws, written and oral, that we believe we received at

Mount Sinai, and the vast literature of commentary and interpretation surrounding those laws. (See: *An Introduction to the World's Biggest Book Club*.)

About the Author

Daniella Levy is a writer, translator, and educator living in Israel with her husband and three sons. Her work has appeared in print and online on several platforms, including Pnima Magazine, Kveller, and Ynet News. She enjoys teaching women's self-defense, learning new languages (which she then refuses to speak), and, as evidenced by the preceding pages, composing unreasonably long e-mails to people.

For more letters to Josep on Judaism and life in Israel, visit the blog at letterstojosep.com, or visit the Facebook page: www.facebook.com/letterstojosep.

Connect with Daniella online:

daniella-levy.com

@DaniellaNLevy

Printed in Great Britain
by Amazon